The
BATTLE
PLAN
for
PRAYER

The
BATTLE
PLAN
for
PRAYER

FROM BASIC TRAINING
TO TARGETED STRATEGIES

STEPHEN & ALEX
KENDRICK

PUBLISHING GROUP
NASHVILLE, TENNESSEE

978-1-4336-8866-9

Published by B&H Publishing Group
Nashville, Tennessee

Dewey Decimal Classification: 248.3
Subject Heading: PRAYER \ SPIRITUAL WARFARE \
CHRISTIAN LIFE

1 2 3 4 5 6 7 8 • 20 19 18 17 16 15

CONTENTS

Introduction 1

Part I: Enlistment

1. The Legacy of Prayer 9

2. The Power of Prayer 15

3. The Priority of Prayer 21

Part II: Basic Training

4. Why: The Ultimate Purpose of Prayer 27

5. What Is and Isn't Prayer 32

6. What: Types of Prayer 40

7. What Are God's Answers to Prayer? 48

8. When: Scheduled Prayer 54

9. When: Spontaneous Prayer 58

10. How: The Postures of Prayer 62

11. How: The Locks of Prayer 67

12. How: The Keys of Prayer 74

Part III: Conditioning

13. Vertical: The Cross of Christ. 80

14. Vertical: Repentance Versus Pride. 91

15. Horizontal: Unity Versus Division. 97

16. Your Heart: Faith Versus Doubt 102

17. Your Heart: Secret Versus Show 108

18. Your Heart: Obedience Versus Rebellion 113

19. Your Heart: Persistence Versus Impatience. 118

Part IV: Strategies

20. The Word of God 125

21. The Will of God 130

22. The "Whatever" from God 136

23. The Wonder of God's Names 143

24. The Wisdom of God 149

25. The Ways of God's Spirit 154

26. Praying Offensively 160

27. Praying Preemptively 165

28. Praying Defensively 172

29. Praying Extraordinarily 180

Part V: Targets

30. Praying for the Lost. 188

31. Praying for Believers. 194

32. Praying for Family 200

33. Praying for Authorities 206

34. Praying for Laborers in the Harvest. 211

35. Praying for Churches and Revival 217

Part VI: Ammunition

Appendix 1: Rhythms of Prayer 224

Appendix 2: Spiritual Temperature Test. 226

Appendix 3: The Gospel. .228

Appendix 4: Prayer Strategy Verses. 232

Appendix 5: Spiritual Ammo 242

Appendix 6: The Names of God. 244

Appendix 7: Starting a Prayer Ministry. 250

Part VII: Reinforcements

Discussion Questions. 252

Battle Plan Resources. 257

The Meaning of the Crosshairs Symbol

THE CROSS in the middle reminds us that successful prayer begins with a relationship with God through Jesus Christ and faith in His shed blood on the cross. (John 14:6, Eph. 3:12; Col. 1:15–20)

THE VERTICAL LINES in the cross, as well as above and below it, remind us to stay vertically aligned with God and His Word in prayer. (John 14:13; 15:7; 1 John 5:14)

THE HORIZONTAL LINES in the cross and on both sides remind us to stay right with others. This includes forgiving, apologizing, and also praying in agreement with others. (Matt. 5:23–24; 18:19–20; Mark 11:25)

THE INNER CIRCLE means to maintain a pure heart in prayer. When you pray, you should keep no unconfessed sin or bitterness in your heart and you should approach God humbly, repentantly, submissively, and in faith. (Ps. 66:18; Mark 11:24; James 4:7–10)

THE CROSSHAIRS remind us to aim our intercession and to pray specifically, strategically, and persistently. (Matt. 7:7–8; John 15:7; James 5:16)

INTRODUCTION

In April 1948, a farmer in a small rural town in south Georgia looked up to see a tornado approaching his property. As he ran for cover, his wife crowded their three young daughters under the dining room table and waited in fear.

When the devastating twister arrived at their house, the little girls watched their mother cry out to God at the top of her voice for protection. Moments later, the deafening, train-like sound of the winds faded into the distance, and then the family walked outside to see the aftermath of the storm.

The destruction was all around them. Their barn a few yards away was heavily damaged. Power lines were down on the ground. The giant oak trees in front of their house were uprooted, now lying on their side, and the church across the street had been rocked off its foundation. But their home and family were left completely untouched.

This farmer and his wife were our grandparents. And their six-year-old daughter, who was greatly impacted by this experience, grew up to become our mother. The three of us, her sons, and our nineteen children would not be here today if God had not protected their family during that storm.

There is power in prayer. We grew up in a praying home, we've attended praying churches, and we've seen God answer countless specific prayers over the years.

When we were in high school, for instance, our father and a few trusted friends believed God was leading them to launch a new Christian school in our area. To get started, of course, they needed desks, books, and the right location. But with little money, what they needed more than anything was faith. And prayer.

During those early days of the school, we watched how God rapidly guided and provided. A local church agreed to house the school and allow their facilities to be remodeled for the purpose. A local business donated free lumber. A volunteer ministry team from Tennessee showed up to help with construction. Within weeks, new classrooms and offices were completed. Another school called and offered books, desks, and chairs.

The timing was unbelievable. Soon we had students sitting in new classrooms, with books in their hands and teachers in front of them. Our father went on to serve as headmaster for two decades, watching the Lord continue to provide what was needed year after year. In the fall of 2014, the school celebrated its twenty-fifth anniversary, having impacted thousands of students and families for Christ through the years.

During the 1990s, when our father needed the funds to rent a modular unit for the school, he prayed that God would somehow provide the seven thousand dollars to set it up. A few days later, a married couple unexpectedly dropped by his office and asked if the school had any needs. Dad shared about the expansion opportunity and how he was praying specifically for the needed amount. Their mouths dropped as they looked at each other in amazement.

The husband said, "Well, we're here because we believe God wanted us to bring this to you." He reached into his pocket and pulled out a check—already made out in the amount of seven thousand dollars!—and laid it on our father's desk. It was to the *penny* what Dad had been praying God would send.

We witnessed answered prayers like these all the time.

In 2002, following in our father's footsteps, we were privileged to launch a Christian movie ministry at our church with no money, no professional experience, and no film school training. But we knew God could provide what we needed. And with the support of our church, we laid every need before Him in prayer. We had to write the scripts, find the right actors, secure the right equipment, pull off the entire production, and then obtain distribution. God provided everything we needed at every level. Each of the five movies we've been part of producing has resulted from a long string of specifically answered prayers. We know we would have failed otherwise.

In our office we've created a "Wall of Remembrance." Numerous framed pictures serve as visual reminders of God's provision, each representing a clearly answered prayer. Among them is a picture of Alex as a young college student with a dream to make movies for the Lord. Another features a two-year-old orphan in Nanjing, China, that God guided Stephen and his wife to adopt. One shows a forklift on a train track that just happened to be nearby one of our movie sets, sitting idle behind a man's house, right when we needed it. One depicts a group of men in Malawi, Africa, holding up resolution commitments to lead their families, after a history in which they'd all but abandoned them. One other picture is of three brothers with their arms around each other, smiling, taken years after our father had prayed we would all be working together someday.

Each picture represents a story of God's faithfulness in our lives. It's overwhelming to see them all together. Incredible provision. Unbelievable direction. Impossible odds. The list goes on.

God has been so gracious and shown His kindness and power in countless ways over the years. Yes, He does it through His creation and His Word. Yes, He does it through changed lives. But one of the most impactful means of His blessing has been through *specifically* answered prayers.

We know prayer works. We can't deny it at this point. And we don't want to.

Answered prayers aren't merely highly unlikely coincidences. They are fingerprints of a living, loving God who invites all of us to draw close to Him, the One who made us and "is not far from each one of us; for in Him we live and move and have our being" (Acts 17:27–28 NKJV). So we echo the apostle John, when he stated, "That which we have seen and heard we declare to you, that you also may have fellowship with us; and truly our fellowship is with the Father and with His Son Jesus Christ. And these things we write to you that your joy may be full" (1 John 1:3–4 NKJV).

That is our hope for this book—that you not only experience the joys of answered prayer more fully, but that you'll get to know God more deeply and fellowship with Him more personally as you travel these pages.

So we invite you to join us—and countless others—on a journey of learning how to pray more biblically and strategically. How to approach God's throne of grace with great freedom and faith. How to more effectively fight the battles of your life in prayer first. How to cast your cares onto the shoulders of One who deeply cares for you.

Together, we'll walk through some of the most important foundational passages and truths in the Bible regarding prayer, and also share many wonderful resources God gives all of us to help us pray with greater power and precision. We'll discuss prayer's benefits, purposes, and how God answers. Then we'll venture through the importance of properly preparing our hearts so we can boldly approach Him in faith. Last, we'll share specific prayer strategies you can use to help you pray more biblically and stand firm during moments of temptation and spiritual attack, ready to better intercede on behalf of others around you.

If you desire to draw closer to God and pray more effectively and strategically, it is no accident you're reading this book. We believe the Lord is calling you into a deeper relationship with Him. And we are cheering you on, daring you to dive in to this journey.

Here at the outset, we challenge you to make a commitment to three things:

First, *READ this book a chapter a day.* We suggest at least five days a week for the next seven weeks, but whatever works for your schedule. Each chapter should only take you around ten minutes to read.

Second, *READ the Bible each day.* Let the Word of God mold you into a person of prayer. We encourage you to read through the Gospel of Luke during these seven weeks and be studying it through the lens of what you can learn from Jesus about prayer. You are also encouraged to look up and study verses in each chapter that you are unfamiliar with that spark your interest.

Third, *PRAY every day.* Prayer should be both scheduled and spontaneous. Choose a place and time when you can pray alone each day, preferably in the morning (Ps. 5:3). Write down specific needs and personal requests you'll be targeting in prayer over the next few weeks, along with the following prayer:

Heavenly Father, I come to You in Jesus' name, asking that You draw me into a closer, more personal relationship with You. Cleanse me of my sins and prepare my heart to pray in a way that pleases You. Help me know You and love You more this week. Use all the circumstances of my life to make me more like Jesus, and teach me how to pray more strategically and effectively in Your name, according to Your will and Your Word. Use my faith, my obedience, and my prayers this week for the benefit of others, for my good, and for Your glory. Amen.

May we each experience the amazing power of God in our generation as a testimony of His goodness for His glory!

MY SCHEDULED PRAYER TIME

___:___ a.m./p.m.

MY SCHEDULED PRAYER PLACE

_____

MY PRAYER TARGETS

Develop a specific, personalized, ongoing prayer list using one or more of the following questions:

- What are your top three biggest needs right now?
- What are the top three things you are most stressed about?
- What are three issues in your life that would take a miracle of God to resolve?
- What is something good and honorable that, if God provided it, would greatly benefit you, your family, and others?
- What is something you believe God may be leading you to do, but you need His clarity and direction on it?
- What is a need from someone you love that you'd like to start praying about?

1. _____

2. _____

3. _____

4. _____

5. _____

6. _____

7. _____

8. _____

9. _____

10. _____

11. _____

12. _____

13. _____

14. _____

15. _____

16. _____

17. _____

18. _____

19. _____

20. _____

1

THE LEGACY OF PRAYER

O You who hear prayer, to You all men come.
(Ps. 65:2)

Prayer can accomplish what a willing God can accomplish. It is a beautiful, mysterious, and awe-inspiring gift. There is no greater privilege for anyone than being able to personally talk with and speak into the ears of Almighty God. There's not an issue we're facing that prayer cannot address because nothing is too difficult or impossible for God to handle. And there is no greater legacy we could embrace or leave behind us than one of faithfulness in prayer.

It should not surprise us, then, to discover that the greatest and most spiritually successful men and women in the Bible were always people of prayer. Abraham walked by faith but was guided by prayer, and the nations of the world have never been the same because of it. Isaac's intercession on behalf of his barren wife resulted in the birth of Jacob, who became the father of the nation of Israel (Gen. 25:21). Moses spoke with God "as a man speaks to his friend," receiving God's guidance and revelation for his leadership decisions (Exod. 33:11). The world still has the Torah and the Ten Commandments as fruit of it.

David talked to God "morning, noon, and night" (Ps 55:17 HCSB) and wrote the longest book in your Bible because of it. The Psalms are filled with a plethora of passionate prayers set to song. Nehemiah's intercessions resulted in Israel miraculously rebuilding the city walls of Jerusalem in incredible time. You can visit this city, as we have, and see a portion of Nehemiah's wall still standing today. Daniel so cherished talking with God that he prioritized it three times a day and was willing to give up his life rather than give up his prayer time.

From Joseph to Jeremiah, Hannah to Hosea, the Scriptures are replete with people who discovered God really does listen and respond to those who approach Him in faith. Elijah was basically a walking example of answered prayer and became an inspiration for New Testament believers (James 5:16–18).

Yet Jesus Christ remains the ultimate model and Master of prayer. At His birth, Jesus and His family were greeted in the temple by Anna, a widow who served God in prayer day and night. At the start of His public ministry, He rose up out of the water at His baptism, the heavens were opened, and the Holy Spirit descended "while He was praying" (Luke 3:21–22).

Before choosing His disciples, Jesus spent all night in prayer to God. As they followed Him, they discovered His private habit was to rise early and pray before the sun rose (Mark 1:35). Even as His popularity was exploding, He would "often slip away to the wilderness and pray" (Luke 5:15–16).

His first fully recorded sermon in the Scriptures explains the fundamentals of how to pray (Matt. 5–7). He taught and challenged His followers to "watch and pray" (Mark 14:38 NKJV) and to pray instead of giving up (Luke 18:1). He angrily threw the money changers out of the temple, shouting, "My house shall be called a house of prayer" (Matt. 21:13).

He gifted the world with the greatest model prayer of all time (Matt 6:9–13) and later prayed the most powerful high priestly prayer of all time (John 17).

Before His betrayal and crucifixion, Jesus knelt alone in the Garden of Gethsemane and prayed so deeply and desperately that His sweat literally became drops of blood (Luke 22:44). Even while suffering in agony on the cross, He prayed out loud three times between His final breaths. Then after ascending into heaven, He sent His Spirit to fill believers and specifically call us to more effective prayer (Rom. 8:15–16). Now as our High Priest, Jesus stands at the right hand of the Father and ever lives to make intercession for us (Heb. 7:23–28).

Andrew Murray wrote, "Christ's life and work, His suffering and death, were founded on prayer—total dependence upon God the Father, trust in God, receiving from God, and surrendering to God. Your redemption is brought into being by prayer and intercession. The life He lived *for* you and the life He lives *in* you is a life that delights to wait on God and receive from Him. To pray in His name is to pray as He prayed. Christ is our example because He is our Head, our Savior, and our Life. In virtue of His deity and of His Spirit, He can live in us. We can pray in His name because we abide in Him and He abides in us."[1]

The launch of the New Testament church and all of Christian history can only be understood through the lens of powerful prayer. Peter constantly relied on it, and Paul was practically addicted to it (Phil. 1:4–5; 1 Thess. 5:17).

The greatest Christian missionaries of all time were also men and women of prayer. Hudson Taylor had an unprecedented impact on China in the late 1800s, resulting from his establishment of the China Inland Mission. He started 125 schools and introduced untold thousands of people to faith in Christ. In a book written by his son and daughter-in-law, they reveal that *Hudson Taylor's Spiritual Secret* was that he obediently walked closely with God in prayer. Howard Taylor wrote of his father, "For forty years the sun never rose on China a single day that God didn't find him on his knees."[2]

In England, a humble man named George Müller led the Ashton Down Orphanage in Bristol and took care of more than ten thousand orphans throughout his life. He did so without ever asking anyone for money. He would pray in secret and then watch God provide in public. When he died, he'd recorded detailed accounts of more than fifty thousand documented answers to prayer in his journals. His example and teachings on prayer have blessed millions around the world.

One of them was England's great preacher, Charles Haddon Spurgeon. Thousands gathered each week to hear the powerful, expository messages of this "Prince of Preachers," who taught and wrote extensively on the power of prayer. When visitors came through his New Park Street Church, he would often walk them to the basement prayer room where people were faithfully on their knees interceding to God for Spurgeon and their community. Spurgeon would declare, "Here is the powerhouse of this church."

In the United States, John Wesley and Jonathan Edwards helped usher in the Great Awakenings in the 1700s that radically changed the culture of America from rampant wickedness to a contagious pursuit of God. Their strategy included preaching God's Word while calling and uniting believers together in sincere, extraordinary prayer.

And these examples are only a drop in the ocean of people through the years who have found and experienced God on their knees.

We have each been given a rich legacy of the power and importance of prayer, both in Scripture and throughout Christian history. Every generation needs courageous believers who will trust God at His Word and pick up the baton of intercession, continuing the powerful legacy of faithfully standing in the gap and seeking His heart in prayer. Our hope is that every chapter of this book will enrich your relationship with the Lord and equip you to walk closer to Him while becoming a more committed and effective prayer warrior for His glory.

No church program, religious event, political effort, or humanitarian cause can trump the awesome power of what God can do in response to the prayers of His people. What would happen if believers and churches today followed the great people of the Bible and in Christian history and began to pray powerfully and effectively? What if we decided to get right with God and begin humbly seeking His face in faith for revival and spiritual awakening like they did during the first and second great awakenings? What might God do through us? Through you?

Are you ready to pray for it?

Father, I come before You and thank You for the great legacy of prayer that has come before us. I ask You to pour out Your Holy Spirit on me and Your church. Draw me into a daily, more intimate walk with You. May prayer become as natural to me as breathing, and may You work through my prayers to help bring about Your kingdom and Your will in my heart, my home, and my generation. In Jesus' name, I pray, amen.

Notes

1. Andrew Murray, *The Ministry of Intercessory Prayer* (Minneapolis, MN: Bethany House, 1981), 106–107.
2. Howard and Geraldine Taylor, *Hudson Taylor's Spiritual Secret* (Chicago, IL: Moody, 2009).

2

THE POWER OF PRAYER

The weapons of our warfare are not of the flesh,
but divinely powerful for the destruction of fortresses.
(2 Cor. 10:4)

Trench warfare was used only sparingly in military craft throughout most of modern history. By the time of the American Civil War in the 1860s, some of the Union and Confederate generals began employing it as a defensive strategy. The increased range and velocity of firearms had reached a high enough level that armies could no longer afford to merely march at one another in columns, taking huge casualties on both sides.

But the heavy, rapid-firing machine guns of World War I left no other option. Digging in and climbing down into trenches became the standard method of survival. Throughout battlefields along the Western Front in Europe, a series of networking foxholes began to emerge on either side of the fighting. From 1914 to 1918, Allied forces dug in against the armies of Germany and the Central Powers. And ugly war slogged on with no end in sight.

The strength of the trenches was protection, but their benefit came at the expense of mobility. When advancing troops would try to make a run on their opponent, the barbed-wire barricades and fortified walls proved difficult to penetrate. Long, arcing shots were about the best they could do. Any attempt at gaining the element of surprise seemed nearly impossible. There was almost no defeating the enemy under these conditions. Just endless fighting. Until . . . the tank.

Great Britain, under Winston Churchill, developed the first military tank in history by engineering an armored car onto the chassis of a farm tractor. Almost like a ship on land. The combination of steel with off-road capability immediately turned the nature of ground fighting from an almost purely *defensive* operation to one of *offensive mobility* . . . and eventually turned the whole tide of the war. The prospect of being able to move actively and thunderously toward the enemy, while being protected during the ride, spelled the end of merely digging in and hoping for the best.

Prayer is our armored tank. And when put into action by God's people, "the gates of hell shall not prevail against it" (Matt. 16:18 KJV). Prayer is our major assault weapon in battle.

The apostle Paul certainly used it in that manner. After listing the various pieces of equipment known as the "full armor of God" (Eph. 6:13), he mentioned prayer as being an equally essential element of spiritual warfare, just like the shield, sword, and helmet. "Pray at all times in the Spirit," he said (v. 18). Prayer, to him, was a forward moving force, a battering ram that powered him ahead in pursuit of God's will. "Pray also for me," he said in the next verse, "that the message may be given to me when I open my mouth to make known with boldness the mystery of the gospel" (v. 19 HCSB). Prayer was the battle strategy he needed to propel him on to victory.

He was actually writing this request from prison, as an "ambassador in chains" (v. 20). Think how many layers of stone-cold reality stood between him and anything resembling the continuation of his ministry. And yet from inside his confined situation, prayer was still blowing holes into every obstacle that stood between him and his next assignment. To be locked up hand and foot, yet be bold enough to consider yourself free and ready to engage in whatever God has in store . . . that's *NOT* how normal people think. Unless we're people of prayer.

Prayer can do anything. Because with God, "all things are possible" (Matt. 19:26). It can reach out and address any issue that anyone is facing anywhere on the earth. It can be silently engaged without the enemy ever hearing the life-changing conversation going on in our heads and hearts with our Commander in Chief.

So this is not just a harmless little church ritual we're talking about. Nor a pitiful beggar asking for a handout he's almost sure he won't receive. There's raw power here. There's access to God Almighty. There's a certainty of His sovereignty. There's a boldness that no amount of enemy resistance can steal from us unless we give it away. And that only happens when we don't pray.

"The effective prayer of a righteous man can accomplish much" (James 5:16). The prophet Elijah, as this same

17

passage in James says, "prayed earnestly that it would not rain, and it did not rain on the earth for three years and six months. Then he prayed again, and the sky poured rain and the earth produced its fruit" (vv. 17–18). Prayer means that God's miracle-working power is always a possible solution to whatever challenge stands before us.

Prayer provides an unlimited spiritual data plan, meaning we never need to worry we've drifted out of range from the signal tower. We can "pray without ceasing," the Bible says (1 Thess. 5:17) and know we're being heard with crystal clear accuracy at all times. Prayer is privileged access to the God of the universe, bought and paid for by the blood of His Son on our account for all those who freely receive Him as Lord.

Paul said making our requests known to God "by prayer and supplication with thanksgiving" (Phil. 4:6) results in an incredible exchange of energy. Instead of staying burdened and overwhelmed by the fear and worry of it all, we're given instead "the peace of God, which surpasses all comprehension" (v. 7). This kind of impenetrable peace operates like an armed guard around our hearts and minds—a peace officer, you might call it—preventing our torqued emotions from making us do things out of fear or desperation. Prayer enables us to rest and trust.

Prayer is like a standing counseling session, 24/7, no appointment necessary. Just walk in. And expect to find your Counselor—which is one of the ways Jesus described the Holy Spirit (John 16:7)—always fully understanding your situation and ready to impart timely wisdom. Even when the truth means confronting us with our sin, the truth also means reminding us of Christ's righteousness, which covers it all with His grace and mercy, as well as the truth about our enemy's certain demise (John 16:8–11). So in prayer, there's no need for any secrets. There's perfect honesty, perfect freedom, perfect forgiveness, and perfect confidence.

Prayer is all these things and more—as we know and will come to see. And because of this, the first observation about prayer is: *Why do we so rarely do it?* With everything that prayer can be to us, why would anyone choose not to pray?

Certainly there's wisdom in working hard and planning and trying to be personally responsible. Those are all good ways of attacking life. But without the addition of prayer to animate these noble qualities with the might and wisdom of God, they don't do much. Prayer is what infuses all our efforts and the genuine concerns of our hearts with God's boundless ability. Prayer is what frames our pressing, short-term issues with God's eternal perspective, showing us just how temporary—and endurable, and winnable—even our most intense battles truly are. Prayer means hope. Prayer means help. Prayer means relief. Prayer means power.

And a lot of it.

Lord, I ask that You forgive me for the times when I haven't valued or believed in the power of prayer that You've offered to me. I've tried making things happen in other ways. But that hasn't often proved so effective. Father, I want to learn to pray in faith. I want to grow closer to You. I want to experience this kind of confidence and freedom to believe You, rely completely on

You, and go into battle with You. Guide me, I pray, as I try to trust You more. Train me. Equip me. Make me a mighty warrior in prayer. Be glorified through me as I trust in You. In Jesus' name, amen.

3

THE PRIORITY OF PRAYER

My prayer came to You, into Your holy temple.
(Jonah 2:7)

 God has strategically chosen to establish and utilize prayer as part of His sovereign plan for us. It is like oxygen to our spiritual lives. It provides the needed wind in our sails to propel everything we do as believers, and it's the unseen key to the success of every ministry of the church.

It allows God's children to interact with our heavenly Father like beloved sons and daughters before their earthly father (Matt. 7:9–11). Prayer aligns the body of Christ with her Head. It's the key to intimacy between the bride of Christ and her Bridegroom. Human frailty, joined in communion with divine perfection. Prayer is simply too wonderful and important not to do it. It's a big deal to God and should be a big deal to us.

But praying isn't always easy. It can feel very counterintuitive to pause when we have so much to do, trying to focus our thoughts in the midst of a million distractions, say *no* to our selfishness and self-sufficiency, and humble ourselves before an Almighty God whom we cannot control and cannot presently see or hear with our physical senses. It seems easier just to go out and attempt to fix things ourselves than to stop and pray about them. So we tend to put it off and save it as an emergency parachute during times of crisis.

But approaching a holy and sovereign God in prayer is something we should prize and never take for granted. We are very needy of God. He created the universe from nothing by the power of His spoken word. We, on the other hand, have never created anything. He is perfect and maintains all authority in heaven and earth, while we stumble in many ways (Luke 9:23; James 3:2). God is dependent on nothing at all, while we are completely dependent on Him every second of every day (John 15:4–5). He knows every detail of everything in all places at all times (Psalm 139:1–18), while we don't know what will happen tomorrow and are already forgetting what we did yesterday.

This is why prayer should be first in the order of things (1 Tim. 2:1–8).

Jesus prioritized prayer above almost everything else. The disciples saw Him continually praying in secret and walking with spiritual power publicly. That's likely why they summarized their seventeen thousand training requests of Him with these words: "Lord, teach us to pray" (Luke 11:1).

He also prioritized it above almost everything else in the church. When He ran the money changers out of the temple, He proclaimed, "Is it not written, 'My house shall be called a house of prayer for all the nations'? But you have made it a robbers' den" (Mark 11:17). With this one violent, surprising motion, He distilled down the purpose of God's house and the meeting together of God's people to a central priority: *believers getting together for prayer*. He did not say, "My house shall be called a house of sermons" or "a house of singing" or "a house of evangelism" or "a house of fellowship." While those things are invaluable and certainly have their place, prioritizing prayer means prioritizing God Himself. It means prioritizing the activity of God above the activity of man. As Jesus well knew, everything else that occupies the church's time and energy will be lacking in power and blessing and the fragrance of God's presence if prayer is not kept first.

Too often, however, we put the cart before the horse by making prayer an add-on. An afterthought. A bonus feature to what we're already doing, placing our own work ahead of God's. But this puts us on a path to eventually becoming dead churches with lifeless worship, featuring well-prepared but powerless sermons, delivered to lukewarm, distracted members who live in sinful defeat and share superficial fellowship with one another. And this, very sadly, is the state of much of the church. It's not because we don't mean well. We do. We work hard. We do our best. But that's part of the problem. God never intended for us to live out the Christian life or accomplish His work on the earth in our own wisdom or strength. His plan has always been for us to rely on the Holy Spirit and live a life of obedience in prayer.

If we were to press the pause button, repent, and move prayer to a place of priority in our families, schedules, and church lives, everything would be ignited and impacted by it. It would be like striking the match before trying to cook over the fire, plugging in the lamp before attempting to flip it on, or cranking up the engine before trying to put the car into gear. We would all worship better, sing better, fellowship better, give better, evangelize better, share better, and behave much better if we were first humbling ourselves, confessing our sins, asking God's Spirit to fill us, and submitting ourselves to Him in prayer.

A deep devotion to prayer was always connected to the success of the New Testament church. Before the Holy Spirit came down in power at Pentecost, the followers of Christ were "all with one mind . . . continually devoting themselves to prayer" (Acts 1:14). The word *devote* carries the idea of *insisting* on something and *clinging* to it. It's the picture of a soldier staying close to his commanding officer.

Faithful. Steadfast. Loyal. Standing guard.

After God's Spirit fell upon them, leading to thousands being saved, the believers were again "continually devoting themselves" to prayer, among other things (Act 2:42). Even when problems arose in the church, such as the widows feeling neglected, the apostles quickly delegated the responsibility to qualified deacons, adding, "But we will devote ourselves to prayer and to the ministry of the word" (Acts 6:4). They just kept sticking to it. This same priority was instilled in the new churches that were being started, and it remains God's Word for us today in our lives and in our churches:

"First of all, then, I urge that entreaties and prayers, petitions and thanksgivings, be made on behalf of all men"

(1 Tim. 2:1). "Be devoted to one another in brotherly love . . . rejoicing in hope, persevering in tribulation, devoted to prayer" (Rom. 12:10, 12). "Devote yourselves to prayer, keeping alert in it with an attitude of thanksgiving; praying at the same time for us as well" (Col. 4:2–4).

Everywhere we turn, prayer should be there to meet us.

And when it does, the following results will begin to show up with increasing regularity. Scripture specifically ties each of these things to prayer. Consider them a sneak preview of what will happen if your church truly becomes devoted to prayer.

- evangelism of the lost (Col. 4:3; 1 Tim. 2:1–8)
- cultivation of discipleship (Luke 11:1–2; John 17)
- true Christian fellowship (Acts 2:42)
- wise decisions (James 1:5)
- obstacles overcome (Mark 11:22–24)
- needs met (Matt. 6:11; Luke 11:5–13)
- true worship ignited (Matt. 6:13; Acts 2:41–47)
- revival sparked (2 Chron. 7:14)

In light of this, read the following description of the early church through the lens of a devotion to prayer and see if it makes much more sense to you. The Word of God, fellowship, and the breaking of bread were all a part of their lives together. But prayer was breathing life into the whole experience.

So then, those who had received his word were baptized; and that day there were added about three thousand souls. They were continually devoting themselves to the apostles' teaching and to fellowship, to the breaking of bread and to prayer. Everyone kept feeling a sense of awe; and many wonders and signs were taking place through the apostles. And all those who had believed were together and had all things in common; and they began selling their property and possessions and were sharing them with all, as anyone might have need. Day by day continuing with one mind in the temple, and breaking bread from house to house, they were taking their meals together with gladness and sincerity of heart, praising God and having favor with all the people. And the Lord was adding to their number day by day those who were being saved. (Acts 2:41–47)

All of us long to be in a place where true friendship and love abounds, where God is honored, and where His power is being made known in and through our lives. Let's pray this happens in the body of Christ again. *It can* . . . if we will devote ourselves to prayer!

Father, forgive us for relying on our wisdom, strength, energy, and ideas rather than abiding in You and seeking You first. Help us lay aside anything that hinders us from pursuing Your best. Help us prioritize prayer and devote ourselves to it in our personal lives, our families, and our churches. Make our churches truly houses of prayer for all nations. Revive us again, O Lord. Help us walk by Your strength and bring You great glory in our generation. In Jesus' name, amen.

4

WHY: THE ULTIMATE PURPOSE OF PRAYER

Whatever you ask in My name, that will I do, so that the Father may be glorified in the Son. (John 14:13)

 Ultimately, all prayer is for the glory of God. The best answer He can give to any prayer is whatever answer brings Him the most glory.

"For His name alone is exalted; His glory is above earth and heaven" (Ps. 148:13).

"Everyone who is called by My name," He says, has been "created for My glory" (Isa. 43:7).

Glory is a word we hear a lot. It sounds familiar, especially in the language of Christian worship, yet we don't always understand what it means. The Hebrew word for *glory* carries the idea of weight and importance. Majesty and honor. So the "glory of the Lord"—a phrase repeated numerous times in the Bible—is when God reveals a glimpse of who He is. Awesomeness on display. Visible evidence of the vast significance of His being. When He reveals His glory, He is unwrapping a measure of His identity—some of His nature, His holiness, His power, His lovingkindness.

God, of course, already possesses the full weight of His glory, in all its forms and expressions. He exists eternally as the Father, Son, and Holy Spirit and is utterly complete within Himself, within this Trinity of the Godhead. Complete fullness, complete joy. He needs nothing else. One who has all authority in heaven and on earth certainly doesn't need *us* (Rom. 9:20–24). And so the mere fact that we're *here* is a testimony to His glory. The fact that He could and would choose to create us, as well as a world and a universe that we could live in, reveals first and foremost, more than anything else, His awesome glory as Creator. The galaxies and stars reveal His attributes as being the work of an awesome, powerful, majestic Creator. That's their job actually. "The heavens declare the glory of God and the firmament shows His handiwork" (Ps. 19:1 NKJV).

But watch what happens. Throughout history, throughout Scripture, we see God unwrapping additional features of His glory, revealing Himself to individuals in ways that are new and unexpected to them. Abraham, for instance, when God told him to offer his only son Isaac as a sacrifice (Gen. 22), had prior knowledge of God as Creator, as a guide, as a faithful promise-keeper. But in the context of this present challenge, God was about to unwrap a new element of His glory in a stunning display.

The Bible's reporting of this event shows Abraham's stoic obedience to what God had said: "Take now your son, your only son, whom you love, Isaac, and go to the land of Moriah, and offer him there as a burnt offering" (Gen. 22:2). But the irrationality of this divine command could not have been lost on him. Isaac was the child of promise

(Gen. 17:21). He was the miracle baby born to a hundred-year-old man and his ninety-year-old wife. To think, after twenty-five years of waiting, after the remarkable birth of this covenant child, that God would order Abraham now to kill him? It made absolutely no sense—the same way some of the events in your life perhaps seem to make no sense. You can't believe, as you pray, that this is happening. *What is God doing?*

He is thinking of His glory. Abraham expected that God would resurrect Isaac if he sacrificed him (Heb. 11:19). But on Mount Moriah, when the angel of the Lord saw Abraham's faith, when he stopped him from sacrificing Isaac, something unknown about God suddenly clicked. When Abraham heard the rustling of a ram in the nearby brush—an animal suitable as a sacrifice in Isaac's place—God was revealing Himself vividly as *Jehovah Jireh*, "The Lord Our Provider." He had kept this part of His glory somewhat hidden until He could reveal it at the exact, perfect moment when He knew Abraham would most value it and worship Him because of it.

God could've demonstrated or shown Himself to be Abraham's provider in another way, at an earlier time. But He chose *this* way, and *this* time, so His glory would be revealed with maximum impact.

This is God's pattern. He makes His glory known progressively in your life—and *through* your life—from one situation to the next.

Every prayer request (and every scenario that triggers a prayer request) is actually an opportunity for us to witness His glory firsthand. Because when He answers, that's what

He's doing. He's wanting us to see what He is like. Our Provider. Our Healer (2 Kings 20:5). Our Sustainer (Ps. 54:4). The One who is wiser than our own wisdom (1 Cor. 1:25). He wants you to know Him as your Creator, Savior, Lord, Provider, Protector, Friend, Counselor . . . and for you to worship Him as such with full appreciation. Not just generally, but personally.

"Lord, show us Your glory," we pray. And we can always be sure He will.

Jesus told the sisters of Lazarus that their brother's sickness would be "for the glory of God, so that the Son of God may be glorified by it" (John 11:4). And He intentionally waited until Lazarus was dead so His power as "the Resurrection and the Life" could be made known in an awesome display (John 11:1–45). It was a defining moment that revealed Jesus' power to everyone who heard about it.

Paul prayed for the church in Thessalonica "that the name of our Lord Jesus will be glorified in you, and you in Him" (2 Thess. 1:12). The reason we do *anything*, Peter said, is "so that in all things God may be glorified through Jesus Christ" (1 Pet. 4:11)—because Jesus is "the radiance of [the Father's] glory and the exact representation of His nature" (Heb. 1:3).

When you pray for something and ask "that the Father may be glorified in the Son" (John 14:13), prepare for Him to do what He knows will bring Him the most glory.

And when He does, your proper response, like Abraham's, should be to worship. This is what's meant by *glorifying* God— valuing and honoring by your thanks and praise the attribute He's just shown you and revealed about Himself. The Lord, in His many dealings with David, had shown Himself to be "a compassionate and gracious God, slow to anger and rich in faithful love and truth" (Ps. 86:15 HCSB)—same as He'd shown to Moses (Exod. 34:6). And David's reaction to this revelation was to "give thanks to You, O Lord my God" and to "glorify Your name forever" (Ps. 86:12).

That leads to a second kind of response: telling others what God has done. David exhorted God's people to "sing of the ways of the LORD, for great is the glory of the LORD. For though the LORD is exalted, yet He regards the lowly, but the haughty He knows from afar" (Ps. 138:5–6). Paul said the revelation of God's grace should "cause the giving of thanks to abound to the glory of God" (2 Cor. 4:15), so that others, too, can see and celebrate how God is being glorified through His work with His people. So when God answers prayer, brag on what He's done and is doing. *It gives Him glory.* Of all the things prayer is and does, its greatest accomplishment—and its greatest joy—is that it allows us, His beloved children, to be part of bringing Him glory. To God be the glory!

Lord, Yours is the kingdom, the power, and the glory forever. Forgive me for seeking my will and desires above Your glory. I've been looking at what I think You should do—what I'd do if I were You. And yet You've shown me that so much more is at stake. You know exactly what You're doing. Your ways are higher than my ways. What I really want, Lord, is that You receive glory from my life. Maximum glory. The full weight of Your glory. Work in my heart and in each of my situations, Lord, so that You are most glorified. In Jesus' name, amen.

5

WHAT IS AND ISN'T PRAYER

As for me, my prayer is to You,
O LORD. (PS. 69:13)

rayer is not about prayer . . . just like a cell phone is not about a cell phone. A phone's primary purpose is not for itself but to serve as a conduit to connect us in relationships. If held up to our ear without engaging another person with it, we're not making it do what's it's been created to do. Likewise, there are activities you can undertake that may look and feel like prayer, but they're not really prayer if God is not truly engaged.

Sitting with your eyes closed and trying to empty your head of all conscious brain activity is not prayer. The "moment of silence" that's somehow supposed to substitute for public praying—in order to appease the sensitivities of civil rights groups—is not prayer.

Repeating words incoherently is not prayer. Crossing your legs and chanting a mantra. Lighting a candle. Keeping someone generally in your thoughts or on your mind. Those are not really prayer either. You may get down on your knees in church with your head bowed, eyes closed, and even speak words out loud that sound like a prayer, but if you're actually performing to impress people, going through the motion, and not talking to God . . . you're not really praying (Luke 18:10–14). Yes, people can pray while doing various things that traditionally indicate prayer, but simply doing them doesn't automatically make them prayer.

Prayer, at its heart, is communicating with God. Reverently and openly. Sincerely. Interacting directly with the magnificent God of the universe who is really there.

The reason such a basic reminder is even needed is because, honestly, we can deceive ourselves with our own performance or forget we're in His presence when we pray. But realize in prayer that we're bowing before the same One who, in John's Revelation, is described like this: "His head and His hair were white like white wool, like snow; and His eyes were like a flame of fire. His feet were like burnished bronze, when it has been made to glow in a furnace, and His voice was like the sound of many waters. In His right hand He held seven stars, and out of His mouth came a sharp two-edged sword; and His face was like the sun shining in its strength" (Rev. 1:14–16).

When John saw Him, "[He] fell at His feet like a dead man" (v. 17). His immediate reflex was awe-struck worship. Fear. Even though Jesus placed His hand on John and said, "Do not be afraid," the fact remained—and remains—that He is no less majestic and jaw-dropping.

If we could only understand what being in the presence of the Almighty is truly like, our mind wouldn't be casually wandering. We wouldn't be drifting in and out of sleep. We'd be fully alert and overwhelmed. All attention held captive. Stunned. Speechless. And when He did speak, we would be humble, reverent, and very careful what came out of our mouths.

A few select servants of God have had opportunities to experience His visible presence. Moses was called by God to come alone up onto Mount Sinai and to enter into the tent of meeting while the people stood outside watching. To be in God's presence was holy. They realized the seriousness of what meeting with God entailed.

And we, too, must realize—in our day—that prayer is serious business. The only reason we've been given the privilege of prayer at all is because Jesus, our "great High Priest," has violently taken on our sin with His own blood and "passed through the heavens" to create a portal of access to the Father (Heb. 4:14).

When building the temple, the ancient Israelites were instructed by God to hang a thick veil or curtain between the inner temple and the most holy place, behind which His presence would visit. Only the high priest was authorized to pass through it once a year on the ceremonial Day of Atonement. But Jesus—our perfect High Priest—is the spotless Lamb of God whose sacrifice was worthy of being accepted as payment for guilt. At the moment of His death, this heavy veil in the temple was split "down the middle . . . from top to bottom" (Matt. 27:51; Mark 15:38; Luke 23:45). As a result, through the atoning blood of Christ, all who receive His forgiveness of their sins by faith, because of His grace, are invited to draw near to God through the "new and living way He has opened for us through the curtain" (Heb. 10:20 HCSB).

Jesus is our mediator. Our go-between. He's like the protective sheathing that insulates a high voltage, live electric wire. Coursing underneath that layer of coating is enough raw energy to easily kill you. But because the Father chose to send the Son to the earth to live a blameless life— where Jesus in human flesh was able to be touched and seen and felt—this blood of Christ shields us from the consuming fire of the holiness of God. Now "we have confidence to enter the holy place by the blood of Jesus" (Heb. 10:19). To be blessed by God's presence rather than dead on arrival (Exod. 33:20–23).

The two of us were once given the opportunity to do fire training with our local fire department in an actual simulation. We experienced the up-close, intense heat that a firefighter can face in enclosed, dangerous quarters. But despite several hundred degrees of heat surrounding us, we were not burned . . . because we were wrapped head to toe in protective gear that could withstand the awesome temperatures.

Yes, "our God is a consuming fire" (Heb. 12:29). Approaching Him in our sinfulness would be like a Popsicle trying to approach the sun. We must always remember how much higher and grander and greater than us He is. But because of Jesus, our High Priest is able to "sympathize with our weaknesses" since He has been "tempted in all things as we are," though never succumbing to sin (Heb. 4:15), and because we as believers are clothed in His righteousness.

Only through Christ are we safe with God.

We should view prayer as the healthy tension between these two companion truths. It is the simultaneous experience of both God's transcendence and His nearness. He is beyond us, beyond all imagination, yet He's closer than the air around us. And so we're invited to pray. "Let us draw near with confidence to the throne of grace" (Heb. 4:16). In Him, our great God is also our great Friend.

That's where we start.

And then here's where we go. In trying to boil down prayer to its most foundational components—to see what prayer is—we've landed on a practical definition. You may be able to craft a better one. We're not saying this is the only way to summarize it. But we share these three statements in hopes they'll be helpful in your spiritual journey.

What is prayer?

Prayer is communion with God in order to . . .

1. *Intimately know, love, and worship Him.* Prayer is about an intimate sharing and fellowship between two loving parties. This is the "Our Father in heaven, hallowed be Your name" dynamic of prayer. Relationship and worship. Prayer is an ongoing, daily way to know God better and better—to comprehend more of who He is and what He does. And the more we know Him and experience Him, the deeper we grow in our respect and love for Him—love that can never match the depth of His love for us (Ps. 63:3–4). Paul's prayer for the church in Ephesus was that they would "be able to comprehend with all the saints what is the breadth and length and height and depth, and to know the love of Christ which surpasses knowledge, that you may be filled up to all the fullness of God" (Eph. 3:17–19). Knowing

Him and loving Him leads to worshiping Him. The natural response to the presence of God is worship. Honor and loving adoration. Dedication and delight. Willing submission. Which leads us back to another purpose of prayer.

Prayer is communion with God in order to . . .

2. *Understand and conform our lives to His will and ways.* Prayer doesn't merely change things; it will change us. As we pray, God reveals His will and ways to us, and then starts to align our hearts and minds with His. We yield to His awesome lordship. Christ is the "head of the body, the church," worthy of being ascribed "first place in everything" (Col. 1:18). We don't ask Him to configure Himself around the way we want to live. No, we bring ourselves up under *His* authority. We say, "Your kingdom come and Your will be done . . . in me and in my life." We follow where *He* leads. "The sheep hear his voice, . . . he goes ahead of them, and the sheep follow him because they know his voice" (John 10:3–4). The more time we spend with God, the more humble, unselfish, and like Jesus we will become. "We all, with unveiled face, beholding as in a mirror the glory of the Lord, are being transformed into the same image from glory to glory, just as from the Lord, the Spirit" (2 Cor. 3:18).

Prayer is communion with God in order to . . .

3. *Access and advance His kingdom, power, and glory.* When we pray, "Give us this day . . . lead us not into temptation . . . deliver us . . ." we are seeking to access God's kingdom resources, for His mighty power to work on our behalf, and for Him to reveal His glory in our situation. God is unlimited in His capacity to accomplish anything. At the same time, we don't just *receive* these things but we seek to

advance them. When we seek first His kingdom, that's when so many other things fall into place (Matt. 6:33). We pray for things that will lead others to submit to His control and give Him the glory due to His name. Those last words of the Lord's Prayer—"thine is the kingdom, and the power, and the glory, for ever" (Matt. 6:13 KJV)—are not just for church and ceremony. They remind us that God is owner of all, ruler of all, and worthy of all. "For from Him and through Him and to Him are all things. To Him be the glory forever. Amen." (Rom. 11:36). Prayer allows us the priceless privilege to not only know Almighty God better, but to join Him in what He is already doing among the nations for His glory.

God has made us able to pray and do this by redeeming us, by forgiving us, by including us in His inheritance, by giving us the Holy Spirit . . . all the things captured in Ephesians 1 that explain to us who we are in Christ. He has given us access to all the resources we need—"according to the riches of His glory" (Eph. 3:16)—so that we can be strengthened within for complete victory and power in serving Him. In prayer we commune with the One who has abundantly, lavishly poured His blessings out on us. We worship Him, we thank Him, we listen, we learn, we serve. Through Christ, we enjoy constant access to Him while being able to know we're devoting our whole lives to what truly matters most.

Again, prayer is not about prayer. It is about a Person— God Himself. When it becomes merely about accessing the provision or protection of God rather than knowing and pleasing the Person of God, then we are getting off track. But when the one goal of our praying is to live in relationship with Him—one on One—He will cause prayer to also help us experience His purposes, His plans, His provision, His protection, and everything else He intends.

All for His glory.

Father, help me never again forget that I am in Your awesome presence when I pray. Help me not enter into it as duty or a mindless activity, the mere repeating of tired words. But help me come with worship, with love, and with a true desire to experience You personally. Help me abandon my own agendas and self-assurances, wanting to be nowhere else except directly aligned with Your will. And may Your kingdom flow right through this heart and home of mine, taking me wherever You want me to go.

THE DEFINITION OF PRAYER

Prayer is communion with God in order to . . .

1. Intimately know, love, and worship Him.
2. Understand and conform our lives to His will and ways.
3. Access and advance His kingdom, power, and glory.

6

WHAT: TYPES OF PRAYER

I exhort first of all that supplications, prayers,
intercessions, and giving of thanks be made
for all men. (1 Tim. 2:1 NKJV)

Creative lists and methods have been developed over the years to help explain different types of prayers, but for our purposes, we will be using what we learned from others years ago: the acronym A.C.T.S.—Adoration, Confession, Thanksgiving, and Supplication.

Any prayer at any moment will likely be one of these four broad types. And over time, if you want your relationship with God to stay in full bloom, your praying should incorporate each of them.

There are no rigid rules here. God gives freedom in prayer to flow in and out of these areas as needed. You can approach Him with only one, or you can integrate them all. And yet together, these four types provide a useful and natural progression as you interact with the Lord.

1. *Adoration* is prayer that praises and worships God. And He is fully worthy of all our praise. In adoration, we're

not necessarily requesting anything from Him; we're merely adoring and honoring Him in our hearts.

We were each created and called to praise God throughout our lives (Eph. 1:5–6; Heb. 13:15). The psalmist wrote, "Let everything that has breath praise the LORD. Praise the LORD!" (Ps. 150:6). Jesus praised His heavenly Father in prayer and presented praise as a first priority of our prayers. He began His model prayer with: "Hallowed be thy name" (Matt. 6:9 KJV)—a front and center acknowledgment of God's holiness. Totally pure and perfect.

Psalm 150 challenges us to praise God with whatever means possible, in all types of places, at all available times. The Hebrew word *hallelujah* is actually a command to *hallel* (praise) *Yah* (the Lord). It's an invitation to enjoy God and express our wonder of the One who is most wonderful. Think of it as practice for eternity.

Every one of us is wired to worship. And we will give our hearts, attention, money, time, and service to whatever we value the most. By worshiping God wholeheartedly with our lips and lives, we get to do the greatest thing in the greatest way for the greatest One. When we are adoring Him silently in our hearts, proclaiming His goodness out loud, or singing a worshipful prayer, "it is pleasant, and praise is beautiful" (Ps. 147:1 NKJV). When we pray in adoration, we stop focusing on ourselves and our storms, and start fixing our eyes on the only One who is fully able to handle any situation or request (2 Cor. 3:18).

When you study praise in Scripture, you will observe people expressing one or more of the following things to God:

- A reminder of who God is: *You are our Creator; You are awesome; Lord of all.*
- A recounting of what He's done: *You rescued us; You saved us; You provided for me.*
- A recognition of His holiness: *There is none like You; You are greater than . . . better than . . . higher than . . . more powerful than . . . anything else.*
- A rejoicing in His name: *We lift up Your name; I praise Your name; we honor Your name.*
- A relinquishing of control: *I love You and give You my life; I surrender to You; all that I am and have is Yours.*

How often do you praise God while praying? How often do you stop asking and just start bragging on Him? How often do you pause to tell Him how incredible He is—that He is the greatest thing in your universe?

In praise we revel in the reality of His majesty. We remember He is perfect, powerful, and precise. We acknowledge He is beyond us, yet He chooses to draw near to us. So we bask in the warmth of His love and lift our voices to worship Him. We're able to view all of life more properly when we've first prioritized praise.

2. *Confession* is prayer that gets honest about sin. Getting right and staying clean before God is necessary to remain close to Him and be effective in prayer. We are all sinners and all stumble in many ways (James 3:2). Yet we are not ready to properly serve God or ask Him for much of anything until we honestly confess and turn from any unaddressed sin in our lives. But when we do, "How blessed is he whose transgression is forgiven, whose sin is covered!" (Ps. 32:1–2).

God's Word, His Spirit, and your conscience will reveal the ungodly things you have done or the good things you should have done (James 4:17). But through the cross of Christ, God has provided a way for anyone to be forgiven. He does not expose sin in us to condemn us but so we can turn from it, turn to Him, and be cleansed (John 3:16–17; Acts 3:19). We will always be tempted to rationalize sin, deny it, or just stubbornly cling to it. But there is no real freedom or joy there, only emptiness and unwanted consequences. "If we say that we have no sin, we are deceiving ourselves and the truth is not in us," but "if we confess our sins, He is faithful and righteous to forgive us our sins and to cleanse us from all unrighteousness" (1 John 1:8–9). That's why Jesus also included "Forgive us our trespasses as we forgive others" (Matt. 6:12 KJV) as part of our model, daily prayer.

King David prayed a passionate prayer of confession after being confronted with his adultery with Bathsheba and the murder of her husband. He said, "Wash me thoroughly from my iniquity and cleanse me from my sin. . . . Against You, You only, I have sinned" (Ps. 51:2, 4). He testified at another time, "I acknowledged my sin to You, and my iniquity I did not hide; I said, 'I will confess my transgressions to the LORD'; and You forgave the guilt of my sin" (Ps. 32:5). Prayer is a daily opportunity to walk in the light (1 John 1:5–7), be honest, deal with our own darkness, and admit to Him—as well as to ourselves—what He already knows to be true. If God says something is wrong, then we should agree with Him in our hearts.

The phrase used repeatedly in Scripture is to "pour out" our hearts before Him (Ps. 62:8). We should freely come to the One whose mercies are new every morning. He is faithful to cleanse. To heal. To restore our fellowship. Not only will your honest confession lead to a fresh experience of His forgiveness, but it will also help you let go of the chains and walk in greater freedom in the future.

3. *Thanksgiving* is God-directed, humbly expressed gratitude. While praise focuses more on who God is, thanksgiving highlights what He has *done* or *is doing*. Just as parents delight in grateful children, we should "magnify Him with thanksgiving," knowing our heartfelt gratitude greatly pleases our heavenly Father (Ps. 69:30). Thanksgiving is priceless, yet it costs us nothing except "the fruit of our lips, giving thanks to His name" (Heb. 13:15 NKJV).

Ungratefulness, however, is very costly and is actually a poisonous sin (Rom. 1:21; 2 Tim. 3:1–5). Jealousy, greed, lust, complaining, theft, envy, and covetousness can all spring from ungratefulness in the heart. Unthankful people are consistently sour in almost all circumstances. They tend to complain about everything, never fully enjoying what they have, yet always wanting more.

That's why developing a grateful heart is a major part of God's agenda. His Word commands it (1 Thess. 5:18), His works demand it (Ps. 106:47), and His Spirit inspires it (1 Cor. 2:11–12). God's grace helps enable any believer anywhere in the world to give thanks in any situation (Ps. 118:21). "For all things are for your sakes, so that the grace which is spreading to more and more people may cause the giving of thanks to abound to the glory of God" (2 Cor. 4:15).

Regardless of the pain and problems faced in life, we each have things to be thankful for. God's Word says, "*In* everything give thanks" (1 Thess. 5:18), while also "giving thanks always *for* everything" (Eph. 5:20 HCSB). Despite all the rotten things, the Bible tells us we should be "overflowing with gratitude" (Col. 2:7). But how?

It goes back to the unchangeable nature of God. The same qualities for which we praise Him create the context for gratefulness. Though the world grows darker, His Word promises goodness and His love never changes. We always have reason to express thanks because He is *always* working through *all* things (even the bad things) for the good of those who love Him (Rom. 8:28–29). So when all logic says there's no way to be thankful, His past faithfulness and constant care, as well as the sacrifice of His Son, remind us we'd be crazy *not* to trust Him. Gratefully. Even now. We look behind us at what we've seen Him do—miracles that have no other explanation, His ordering of events with impeccable timing—and we see, from the rising to the setting of the sun, great is His faithfulness.

Imagine if you were Joseph serving in the midst of slavery, Daniel standing in the lions' den, David being taunted by Goliath, or Mary watching Jesus being crucified—and asking yourself, "How can I thank God for *this*?" Yet in each of these dark and painful moments, God was working amazingly for their good and would be greatly glorified through the details of those circumstances. So by faith we, too, can stay thankful in prayer. The darkness is only temporary. But salvation, His Holy Spirit, His Word, His love . . . all are eternal. If God did nothing else for us, what He has already done is cause enough for a thousand lifetimes of thanks.

4. *Supplication* is asking for something from God. It means to beseech, petition, or appeal for Him to do or provide something for yourself or others (Eph. 6:18). The Bible says, "You do not have because you do not ask" (James 4:2).

Jesus said to His followers, "Ask, and it will be given to you; seek, and you will find; knock, and it will be opened to you. For everyone who asks receives, and he who seeks finds, and to him who knocks it will be opened" (Matt 7:7–8). We're invited—even commanded—to come and pray, to seek and find.

Yet among these four types of prayer, there's biblical wisdom in listing supplication last. Our hearts are more pure and ready to pray in faith when we have first adored God, confessed our sins, and thanked Him for what He's done.

One important type of supplication is *intercession*, which carries the idea of intervening with a request on behalf of someone else. Interceding is one of the most loving things you can do for others. When God was about to judge Israel, Moses interceded and asked for mercy. While Haman was planning to destroy the Jews, Esther interceded in prayer and then politically interceded for the people and saved her nation. The Bible says Jesus is at the right hand of the Father ever interceding for us (Rom. 8:34), and the Holy Spirit is in the hearts of believers interceding for us according to the will of God (Rom. 8:27). We, too, must learn to pray for others.

A.C.T.S.—Adoration, Confession, Thanksgiving, Supplication. You don't need to always include every type of prayer when you pray. Sometimes you need to just get to the point, like Peter when he cried, "Lord, save me" (Matt. 14:30), or when Jesus said, "Father, glorify Your name," and that was it (John 12:28).

But as you think about your times with the Lord, how often do you weave all four types of prayer into them? Are you heavier in one aspect, yet almost nonexistent in others? Seek a balance and learn to go deeply into *all* of them. Together, they make prayer a richer, more complete experience.

> *Father in heaven, I praise Your name as holy and to be honored. I worship You as my God and ask that You glorify Yourself in my life. Search me and cleanse me of anything that displeases You. Forgive me as I forgive others. Thank You for Your provision, protection, and faithfulness in my life. Thank You for inviting me into Your presence daily. Teach me to pray, O Lord. Train me to joyfully bow in worship, to freely confess any and all sin. I thank You with a humble heart, praying this for myself and also for those closest to me. All to Your Glory, O God! In Jesus' name I pray, amen.*

7

WHAT ARE GOD'S ANSWERS TO PRAYER?

I sought the LORD,
and He answered me. (Ps. 34:4)

God answers prayer. That's not just a slogan. "Everyone who asks receives," Jesus said (Matt. 7:8). But even as a loving father filters the requests of his children, God considers our requests through the lens of His perfect will. Often He responds with something that will prove to be far better than what we'd been wanting.

But He does answer. In His own wise way. In order to show forth His glory. "No good thing does He withhold from those who walk uprightly" (Ps. 84:11). "He who did not spare His own Son, but delivered Him over for us all, how will He not also with Him freely give us all things?" (Rom. 8:32).

In fact, what may surprise you to know is how many of God's answers to prayer, when you pull them out and look at them under better spiritual lighting, are a variation of yes. But in general terms, His answers to prayer form up under about five different types. Let's look at them.

1. *Yes, immediately.* Sometimes when we pray, our request is exactly in line with His will, with His timing, and His answer arrives on the spot. The same day we pray it. But sometimes God's response is even quicker than *that* . . . when He says, "before they call, I will answer" (Isa. 65:24). Think of the servant of Abraham, when he was on mission to find a wife for his master's son Isaac. The man prayed that God would "grant me success today" (Gen. 24:12), hoping for a specific sign that would soon alert him to the right girl. "Before he had finished speaking" (v. 15), a young woman named Rebekah appeared. And in answer to his prayers, she offered to water his camels. Later she would become Isaac's beloved wife.

What does that mean then? She likely started out on her way to the well long before Abraham's servant had begun praying. And what's more, the kind demeanor she displayed, which verified what he'd come looking for, had been developing over her lifetime, already prepared for this divine encounter. God is simply not bound by time. He may start answering a request ten years before you pray it. He's likely already preparing things right now for prayers you will one day pray. It's always a joy to experience an immediate yes.

2. *Yes, in due time.* A delay should not be interpreted as a denial. If a nine-year-old girl asks her mom for a wedding dress she saw, the answer to her request might sound like a *no.* But it's actually more of a "Yes, I'll get you a wedding dress, honey. But not now. You're not ready for it yet."

Zechariah the priest had prayed many times for a child in the earlier years of his life, when his wife continued to prove infertile. But the years had come and the hope had gone. The two of them were now both old, far past the season of childbearing. Yet one day, while serving in the temple, Zechariah received the stunning announcement that "your petition has been heard, and your wife Elizabeth will bear you a son" (Luke 1:13). It may have been decades since the last time he'd offered that prayer. But in all those years when he figured he'd been told *no,* God was working behind the scenes, waiting for a more perfect moment to unveil His amazing *yes.*

Think about Joseph in Egypt, languishing in prison, falsely accused, wanting to be released. Think about the cries of Israel throughout the Old Testament, awaiting their promised Messiah. Think about us today, echoing the prayer of John the apostle—"Come, Lord Jesus" (Rev. 22:20)—desiring God to show up in glory and make His final rescue, taking us to heaven with Him. Yes, He's going to do that. But perhaps not today. What He'll give us *today,* if we'll receive it, is the faith and patience to wait until the right time gets here. This is why we should never let yesterday's seemingly unanswered prayers stop us from praying again today and tomorrow with just as much freedom and faith.

3. *Yes, so you'll learn from it.* Sometimes God, deciding we might learn from the lesson, does go ahead and give us what we ask—realizing we don't really know what we're asking. The people of Israel, embarrassed at not having a king like the other nations around them, demanded that their leader Samuel give them one. He tried to tell them what the Lord had said to him—how a king would conscript their sons and daughters for his whims and desires, tax the people, and take from them without any justification. "Then

you will cry out in that day because of your king whom you have chosen for yourselves," Samuel said (1 Sam. 8:18). But, *no!* They protested. *Give us a king!* And so God gave them King Saul—who made all of God's predictions come true.

We are much better off trusting Him to give us what we need, when we need it, and when we're ready for it. There are moments when, if He gave us what we asked for, we would one day regret it. We would thank Him for saying *no*. We should learn to pray as Jesus did, freely adding to our prayers, "nevertheless not My will, but Yours, be done" (Luke 22:42 NKJV).

4. *No, because your heart's not right.* James said the reason for a delay in God's answer is not always simply a timing issue. Sometimes "you ask and do not receive, because you ask with wrong motives, so that you may spend it on your pleasures" (James 4:3). If lust, greed, bitterness, or pride is at the heart of a request, God may veto an answer in order to guard us from the hurt or idolatry that could result from the toxic request.

The first chapter of Proverbs says, "They will call on me, but I will not answer; they will seek me diligently but they will not find me, because they hated knowledge and did not choose the fear of the LORD" (vv. 28–29). Their attitude and behavior—the true condition of their hearts—stood between their request for help and its arrival. If they were ready to listen, however, if they would repent, the situation could be very different.

Wise mothers and fathers will often withhold a desired privilege in order to get through to their child's heart. They're not saying *no* forever. But they realize their son or daughter is not in a position to appreciate the gift or handle it well. Receiving it would merely worsen the situation. And because God loves us, He may say *no* for the same reason. Remember, if it's not God's will, you wouldn't really want it, not if you knew all that He knows.

5. *No, I've got a better plan.* Sometimes we ask too small. Confined by our limited knowledge, not thinking outside what we've already seen and experienced, we pray for a handful when God wants to give us a houseful.

The lame man who encountered Jesus at the pool of Bethesda, where the sick gathered in hopes of being healed in its mystical tide, wished for some way to be taken down there when the water stirred. "Do you wish to get well?" Jesus asked (John 5:6), cutting to the chase. But all the man could imagine needing was just some chance to get into that pool ahead of the others. Jesus said to Him, in so many words, *Why don't I just heal you right here?* "Get up, pick up your pallet and walk" (v. 8). God decided to give the sick man more than he'd asked for.

Martha, upset at Jesus' delay in arriving so He could do something about Lazarus's illness, said to Him, "Lord, if You had been here, my brother would not have died" (John 11:21). But Jesus knew raising his friend from the dead would be a far better answer and bring the Lord even more glory.

In this situation, His answer was technically a *no*, but it's hard not to call it a super-sized *yes*. An upgrade. We're allowed to pray big prayers, realizing that in asking for things over our heads, God may just choose to totally amaze us even further. That's why it's good to pray, "Lord, would you do more than I can ask or imagine in this situation?" knowing that's exactly what He is able to do (Eph. 3:20 NIV).

Obviously, people can die whom you've prayed would be healed. The job you want can pass you by. Your desire to marry someone or have kids may never come to fruition. Until an answer is final, keep asking in faith. But if the final is not what you hoped, you can trust that God's Spirit will sustain you, and He is benevolent in His omniscience. He is always working all things together for good to those that love Him (Rom. 8:28). You can ask and know with total confidence He will provide exactly what is needed.

But don't forget that many times the only reason why we don't have something from Him is because we never asked in the first place (James 4:2). Even if God said *no* or *not yet* 50 percent of the time, we should not let that stop us from asking and hearing a *yes* with all the rest!

Father, my default has been to think You probably weren't listening. And even if You were, You'd probably say no. I bow before You today—more convinced than ever that I am in wise, loving, caring, powerful hands. Convinced that I can trust You. Convinced that every no is in some way an even better yes. You said You withhold no good thing from those who love You. Thank You for letting me ask, and thank You for letting me know that Your desire is truly for my ultimate good. May I trust You even more and pray with even greater faith knowing You want to be glorified through my answered prayers. In Jesus' name, amen.

WHEN: SCHEDULED PRAYER

After bidding them farewell, He left for
the mountain to pray. (Mark 6:46)

There are times in life when you will be *motivated* to pray. It may be because of a crisis, a hope, or a fear that feels all-consuming. But prayer should also be something that's part of your daily schedule. And not just before meals or when going to bed. We're talking about a time set aside solely to focus on the Lord and your relationship with Him. That's our target for this chapter: *scheduled prayer.*

In 1 Thessalonians 5:17, we are encouraged to "pray without ceasing." This means never being far from the attitude or action of talking and listening to God. Prayer should be a natural part of our thinking. Not just in our worship but in our work. Not just in our quiet moments but also in our chaos. We pray because He's there. We pray because He's God. We pray because He cares.

But this doesn't mean we're sinning if we're not praying every second of every day. That would be impossible. But if we were to say that kids *play constantly* or that teenagers *text their friends constantly*, we wouldn't mean they never do anything else except playing or texting nonstop. We'd just mean that throughout the day, kids are often trying to integrate play into what they're doing. Many teens communicate hourly with their friends through text messages. Likewise, God desires that prayer become an ongoing opportunity we take full advantage of—quietly praising, thanking, and leaning on Him at any moment and context in our minds and hearts.

Interestingly, the Bible connects prayer to the burning of incense before the Lord. Revelation 5:8 says the golden bowls of incense in heaven are "the prayers of the saints." David also wrote, "May my prayer be counted as incense before You; the lifting up of my hands as the evening offering" (Ps. 141:2).

To see what this analogy really means, look back to God's original instructions about the altar of incense, which was located inside the tabernacle: "Aaron shall burn fragrant incense on it; he shall burn it every morning when he trims the lamps. When Aaron trims the lamps at twilight, he shall burn incense. There shall be perpetual incense before the LORD throughout your generations" (Exod. 30:7–8).

That's the manner in which we should look at prayer. It's a crucial part of the life of a believer. It's a priority and a passion.

But along with this "constant" attitude of prayer should be times when we commit to pray as part of our regular schedule. These are times when we intentionally focus ONLY on prayer, not just as an added part of our other daily activities. It's when we say with our actions and priorities that God is above everything else in our lives. In fact . . . He *IS* life.

The lighting of incense was a part of the daily habit and schedule of the priests. Though it burned throughout the day, it was scheduled to begin at the start of their day and would later wrap up at night. We, too, must make prayer a scheduled part of our lives.

Even with his responsibilities as king, David said, "Evening and morning and at noon I will pray" (Ps. 55:17 NKJV). In like manner, Daniel went to his room, opened his window, and routinely prayed to God three times a day, even when praying at such an expected time could mean losing his life. His enemies knew when to be watching for him. And in Mark 1 and Luke 5, we find Jesus getting up early as part of His routine to spend time in prayer.

Whether you're the CEO of a business or between jobs, you should still prioritize prayer as a necessity in your schedule each day. Married couples should schedule a time to pray together. Families should make prayer a part of their normal routine. And churches need scheduled prayer times and prayer meetings within their own congregations, as well as in partnership with other churches in their city.

When we schedule something, we're less likely to forget it or treat it as something we'll "get around to later." After a while, it becomes a routine, then a sacred habit.

That's the goal when scheduling prayer.

Anything important enough to us will be something we make time for. Even when we're extremely busy. But remember, Jesus was busier than all of us, and He prioritized daily prayer.

What if the richest man in your city called you today and said he would give you ten thousand dollars in cash every morning if you showed up and rang his doorbell at 6:00 a.m.? Would you be there? Absolutely. No question. Why? Because if we really want something bad enough and value it enough, we make it happen. We figure out a way to fit it into our schedules. At the same time, our Savior, Jesus Christ, is daily offering us eternal treasures from His Word and the opportunity to talk with His Father, the God of the Universe, to share our hearts and needs. And yet we still come up with excuses as to why we don't have time to make it work.

So determine today that prayer will be the priority God wants it to be in your life. Choose to start each day in prayer. To end each day with prayer. Even better, couple it with time in God's Word. Whether it's an hour or just fifteen minutes, schedule time to be with the Lord, and watch what He does with it in your life.

Lord, when I look at my average day, I see a lot of things that I never consider not doing or making time for. Each day. Every day. And yet prayer—why can I so easily decide not to block out a set time for something this essential? Help me not continue to make this mistake. Thank You for always being here, ready to communicate with me. I commit, Lord, to being there to communicate with You.

9

WHEN: SPONTANEOUS PRAYER

*Let everyone who is godly pray to You in a time
when You may be found. (Ps. 32:6)*

 When we commit to scheduled prayer on a daily basis, we position ourselves to seek and hear from God at a deeper level. But in addition to this priceless time each day, unplanned events give us the opportunity to respond to life with prayer at a moment's notice. Like a soldier who's been given his marching orders at the start of the day, we must be ready to engage whatever comes at us once we're on the battlefield. This is when we learn to use *spontaneous prayers*.

They're all different shades and colors of prayer. Yet they're all prayer. It may be thanking God when you're grateful for an unexpected blessing, or asking His help for someone you've just heard is in a crisis. It may be for wisdom and clarity in making a financial decision, or for the courage to share your faith with a neighbor. When prayer becomes your immediate reflex instead of your last resort, the whole battlefield begins to tilt in your direction.

So as you engage with life, let these things prompt you to pray.

1. *Newness.* Take time to pray whenever you begin something new. Pray at the start of each day, for example. Dedicate it to God, asking for His cleansing, protection, and guidance. Do the same at the start of each new year, new job, or new relationship. We find the men and women of God doing this throughout Scripture. Joshua dedicated the new land of Israel to God (Josh. 3). David did it when Jerusalem became the new capital (2 Sam. 6:17). And King Solomon prayed and dedicated the new temple to God (1 Kings 8). So whether it's a new vehicle, a new house, or a new season of life, take time to pray and dedicate it to the Lord.

2. *Needs.* We serve a God who is in the need-meeting business. Whenever you discover a physical, emotional, or spiritual need, you should allow that need to prompt you to pray. He is *Jehovah Jireh*, the God who provides. Matthew 6:8–11 reminds us that God knows what we need even before we ask Him. But we should still pray in faith, asking Him to meet our needs.

3. *Blessings.* As God provides, protects, forgives, and guides you . . . thank Him! Don't let the routine blessings you receive each day be taken for granted. First Thessalonians 5:18 says, "In everything, give thanks." Ephesians 5:20 adds that we should "always [give] thanks for all things in the name of our Lord Jesus Christ." God is pleased when we remain grateful and humble before Him. Take time to say *Thank You!*

4. *Burdens.* They come in many forms, but all should be taken to the Lord. You may be carrying one yourself or know of someone who is struggling with one. From cancer to divorce, burdens can crush the spirit. Galatians 6:2 tells us to "carry one another's burdens; in this way you fulfill the law of Christ" (HCSB). Let any burden prompt you to pray to the One who loves you and can make it lighter.

5. *Crisis.* Every one of us will eventually face times of crisis. These are not just small burdens but life-changing events. They should also be times when we immediately turn to prayer. Psalm 50:15 says, "Call upon Me in the day of trouble; I shall rescue you, and you will honor Me." God's actions may not look like we think, but He knows what is best and what can bring Him honor. It may be a miracle or comfort in tragedy that leads to God receiving glory. But in either case, He tells us to cry out to Him.

6. *Worries.* When worry washes over you, turn it into prayer. Philippians 4:6–7 reminds us not to be anxious or worried about anything but to go to the Lord in prayer. First Peter 5:7 also says to cast your cares on Him because He cares for you. So when panic or fear try to invade your thoughts, respond by turning each one into a prayer to the God who sees and knows what you're facing, and who also has the solution.

7. *Sin.* Anything related to sin should prompt us to pray. Whether we're being tempted or have already crossed the line, we should immediately turn to the Lord. Jesus instructed His disciples to pray when tempted. God won't allow more than you can handle. But if you've sinned and need forgiveness, 1 John 1:9 has good news. If you humble

yourself and confess your sin, God will forgive and cleanse you. But this prayer should reflect a sincere attitude of repentance and a commitment not to do it again.

Allowing our circumstances to launch our prayers keeps us in the strategic position of encountering God's response. Like Nehemiah, who had the arduous task of rebuilding the protective wall around Jerusalem, we may feel overwhelmed, lacking in support, or even attacked by those opposed to us. But if we respond as Nehemiah responded, we position ourselves to see our powerful God do what only He can do.

Nehemiah prayed at every turn—for favor, for wisdom, for help, for strength, for deliverance, and for victory. And although he was up against incredible odds, he protected Jerusalem by rallying the people and rebuilding the wall in record time. God blessed him and answered his prayers as only God could.

Remember, the topics you can pray for are ANYTHING and EVERYTHING. So keep your spontaneous prayers at the ready, and launch them to the Father as often as you like. He's listening.

Heavenly Father, I do want prayer to be my first response to every situation that occurs in my life. Instead of worrying, instead of complaining, instead of taking credit, instead of celebrating without You, teach me to come to You before going anywhere or to anyone else. What a comfort to know I can never be in a place that You're not already there to hear me and help me. I intend to be in that place more often myself.

10

HOW: THE POSTURES
OF PRAYER

*Come, let us worship and bow down, let us kneel
before the LORD our Maker. (Ps. 95:6)*

 Prayer is not dependent on certain decibel
levels or body positions. God's clear empha-
sis is not on externals but on the heart. And
yet He's created us to be a complete, unified
whole—body, soul, and spirit. All of our various components feed and affect all the others.
We hear of professional golfers who study with coaches to
make even slight alterations in their stance or grip, hoping
to achieve another fifteen yards off the tee or better control
around the greens. How much more should we study the
Word to see how our posture might intensify our praying?

Bowing. To bow, for example, is a physical expression of honor and allegiance. In the second of the Ten
Commandments—an admonition against serving or creating
other gods—the Lord said, "You must not bow down to them
or worship them" (Exod. 20:5 HCSB). The action of bowing is
associated with worship. Even just the bowing of our heads

communicates to our mind that we're addressing the One to whom we've pledged our complete loyalty. When the Lord came down in a cloud around Moses on Mount Sinai, "Moses made haste to bow low toward the earth and worship" (Exod. 34:8). King David, centuries later, said, "As for me . . . I will bow down in reverence for You" (Ps. 5:7). Bowing is an appropriate posture of prayer.

Many other biblical references speak of dropping to our *knees* in prayer. Solomon's monumental prayer at the dedication of the temple was given while he "knelt down in front of the entire congregation of Israel" (2 Chron. 6:13 HCSB). Daniel, even at the risk of death for defying the king's order against praying to anyone other than the king himself, "continued kneeling on his knees three times a day" at the open window of his home, "praying and giving thanks before his God" (Dan. 6:10). And one day, we're told, "*every* knee will bow" before Christ—"in heaven and on earth and under the earth" (Phil. 2:10)—even those who refused to kneel before Him.

Lying prostrate. Sometimes bowing our heads or bowing on our knees still doesn't quite reflect the devotion we intend. When Ezra the priest gave an all-morning, public reading of the law to the returned exiles in Jerusalem, "they bowed low and worshiped the LORD with their faces to the ground" (Neh. 8:6). Jesus, agonizing in the Garden of Gethsemane before His torture and death, "fell on His face and prayed" (Matt. 26:39). And when John later saw Him in His resurrected, glorified form—as described in the apostle's Revelation on the island of Patmos—he admitted he "fell at His feet like a dead man," totally prostrate before the power of God (Rev. 1:17).

Yet just as prayer often drives us lower to the ground in bowed surrender, it also pulls us up, raising us from our earthbound existence.

Lifted hands. Many prayers from Scripture were made with uplifted hands. The idea of folding our hands, while meaningful, is actually more recent in history. But the Bible does talk about raising our hands—"the lifting up of my hands as the evening offering" (Ps. 141:2). Paul said, "I want the men in every place to pray, lifting up holy hands, without wrath and dissension" (1 Tim. 2:8). Both Solomon and Ezra, whom we mentioned earlier, prayed while falling to their knees and lifting their hands—at the same time—a position of total, physical worship and praise.

Lifted eyes. While closing our eyes is a good way of limiting distractions and maintaining focus in prayer, a common biblical expression was lifting the eyes toward heaven, like when Jesus "raised His eyes" before praying at the tomb of Lazarus (John 11:41), or when "looking up to heaven" as He blessed the five loaves and two fish before multiplying them for the crowd of five thousand (Luke 9:16).

Silence. Beyond physical postures, what we do with our voices in prayer is also important. Sometimes the best thing we can do in prayer is be still and know that He is God . . . without saying a word (Ps. 46:10). When awed and amazed, one is often in silence. Psalm 62:1 says, "My soul waits in silence for God only; from Him is my salvation." Psalm 4:4 speaks to silence also: "Meditate in your heart upon your bed, and be still." When the Bible described the prayer of Hannah, in anguish as she prayed for God to give her a child, "she was speaking in her heart, only her lips were moving, but her voice was not heard" (1 Sam. 1:13). No one could hear her silent prayer. But God did. And answered her request.

Lifted voices. Along with lifted hands and lifted eyes, the Bible also exhorts us to lift our voices to the Lord in prayer. "Give ear to my voice when I call to You," David prayed (Ps. 141:1). "My voice rises to God, and He will hear me" (Ps. 77:1).

Crying out. "Evening and morning and at noon I will pray, and cry aloud" (Ps. 55:17 NKJV). This *crying out* is a frequent descriptor of prayers spoken in the Bible. Jesus, we're told, during His life on the earth, "offered prayers and appeals with loud cries and tears to the One who was able to save Him from death, and He was heard because of His reverence" (Heb. 5:7 HCSB). Various translations of the original words for *crying out* carry the idea of shrieking in pain, or making a sound like an animal in danger, or wailing with deep emotion of spirit. It's intense and loud. Heavy and heartfelt. Nearly half of the times when John's Revelation talks about words being spoken in heaven, they're explicitly identified as a "loud voice"—twenty times in its twenty-two chapters.

Again, posture isn't everything. It's not mandatory or specifically prescribed. But we all can identify the difference, can't we, between the prayers we make while flat of our backs, fighting sleep—and the prayers we make while deliberately kneeling, or raising our hands, or speaking aloud. Our body sends signals to the rest of our system, reminding us we're truly in His presence. Truly dependent on Him. Truly His servant. Truly worshipful. And if anything can help us stay this anchored and concentrated on Him, can it really be insignificant?

Consider your own postures of prayer. See how they affect the nature and clarity of your praying. If your religious background, culture, and personal temperament lean toward a particular style—whether quiet and reserved, or loud and demonstrative—think about employing one or more of these biblical postures, perhaps one that's somewhat different from your usual method. Ask God to use it as a way of helping you recognize some previously unnoticed aspects of His character. Helping you further develop your relationship. Helping you strengthen your confidence in Him. Helping you focus your praying so you're not just talking in general but staying on subject. Deliberate and specific. Small adjustments can often yield substantial changes and results.

Lord, take all of me—my hands, my eyes, my feet, my voice. Use all of these gifts You've given me so they return to You as clear expressions of my worship, love, devotion, and submission. I so easily lose sight of You, going through the motions of religion. Lord, turn even my posture of prayer into a means of steadying my wandering mind and opening my ears to Your voice.

11

HOW: THE LOCKS OF PRAYER

Surely God will not listen
to an empty cry. (Job 35:13)

 Accessing God through prayer is not meant to be like cracking a safe. He hasn't hidden the combination so that all we can do is *hope* to land on the right coordinates—otherwise we're blocked out. And yet because He knows everything and understands the dynamic of His holiness versus our sinfulness, God Himself decides and directs us regarding how prayer works, not us. At the same time, life on earth is an unavoidable battle "against the rulers, against the authorities, against the world powers of this darkness, against the spiritual forces of evil in the heavens" (Eph. 6:12 HCSB). God has graciously, protectively given us rules to help our prayer and our warfare be successful.

"I will not leave you as orphans," Jesus said to His followers (John 14:18). He didn't want His disciples left alone to the wolves like an abandoned child without anyone to care for them and lead them. So God in His Word delivered some rules of engagement to make us rough, tough, and battle ready for the difficult days ahead. Think of them not as boxes to check off and follow, but as guides that show us how to transform prayer into a truly rewarding experience. Think of them as expert training tips from a master Teacher whose desire is to send us out there fully prepared, never caught off guard, moving bravely into attack position.

Over the years, we've categorized twenty of these biblical principles into what we call the "Locks and Keys" of prayer. Ten of them are principles that bog down our praying and restrict its freedom and effectiveness. The other ten, however, give prayer a burst of second wind and third wind, pushing it beyond all limits. In this chapter, we'll look at the ten locks of prayer.

1. *Praying without knowing God through Jesus.* Prayer is obviously a fairly universal response when a person is under heavy attack. How many interior hallway closets have turned into prayer closets when a tornado is bearing down? God, of course, can answer any request He chooses from any person who asks. But when it comes to knowing God as Father and walking with Him in answered prayer, Jesus said, "I am the way, and the truth, and the life; no one comes to the Father but through Me" (John 14:6). Just as people who don't share much common ground in their relationship have a hard time keeping conversation going, those who haven't believed in God for the forgiveness of their sins cannot expect God to feel obligated to respond.

2. *Praying from an unrepentant heart.* The Bible says God "knows what we are made of, remembering that we are dust" (Ps. 103:14 HCSB). He's not surprised by our struggle

to remain steadfast. But He also looks at our hearts, and He knows when we are "broken" by our sin (Ps. 51:17). The trouble comes, however, when our hearts aren't broken at all—when we're cold and indifferent toward His Word and our transgressions of it. As the writer of Psalm 66 said, "If I had cherished sin in my heart, the Lord would not have listened" (v. 18 NIV). When we cling to our sin and stiff-arm God, then He will stiff-arm our prayers until we are willing to repent. If we're determined to be the one who calls the shots in our lives, we shoot ourselves in the foot as far as our prayer is concerned.

3. *Praying for show.* People who pray merely to impress others had better enjoy those people's "amens" and compliments while they last. Because according to Jesus, that's the full extent of the reward. "When you pray," He said, "you are not to be like the hypocrites; for they love to stand and pray in the synagogues and on the street corners so that they may be seen by men. Truly I say to you, they have their reward in full" (Matt. 6:5). Public prayers that have not been seasoned by private prayers are hardly worth the hot air required to speak them. Always remember, even when you're leading others in prayer, you're still addressing an audience of One.

4. *Praying repetitive, empty words.* Prayer can take a lot of forms. It can be spoken off the cuff. It can be written out and read word for word. It can be so deep and heartfelt that it only comes out as single syllables. One thing that makes our praying land with a thud of wasted words is when we're talking and talking but aren't even listening to what we're saying. Jesus said, "When you are praying, do not use meaningless repetition as the Gentiles do, for they suppose that

they will be heard for their many words. So do not be like them; for your Father knows what you need before you ask Him" (Matt. 6:7–8). Sure, there's discipline and duty behind prayer. We don't always feel like praying, even when we do it. But we all know when we've let prayer devolve into nothing but canned, thoughtless, mindless words. And no one—not even God—likes to be on the receiving end of that kind of thoughtless conversation.

5. *Prayers not prayed.* Surely the most ineffective prayers of all are those we never even take the time to pray. As James said, "You do not have because you do not ask" (James 4:2). How many times do we just motor past Him, never braking for directions or advice, too busy and in too much of a hurry to stop and seek His counsel? We meant to pray. We thought about it. But we were never able to work it into our schedule. Therefore, we should not expect an unprayed prayer to receive anything other than unsatisfying silence.

6. *Praying with a lustful heart.* Some of us never outgrow our tendency to ask God for things we want only because we think they'll be our source of happiness rather than Him. "You ask and do not receive," James said, "because you ask with wrong motives, so that you may spend it on your pleasures" (James 4:3). If lust, greed, bitterness, or pride are motivations for requesting something, then God will not be pleased to respond. Like a wise parent with a pushy child, God knows what to give us for our good . . . and what not to give us for our good as well. But if we love Him most, then He takes delight in giving us good things we desire. Psalm 37:4 says, "Delight yourself in the LORD; and He will give you the desires of your heart."

7. *Praying while mistreating your spouse.* When we're not treating with love and respect the one person in our life whom we've vowed to treat with love and respect, God makes special mention of it as an inhibitor to prayer. His warning is primarily to men: "Husbands . . . live with your wives in an understanding way . . . and show her honor as a fellow heir of the grace of life, so that your prayers will not be hindered" (1 Pet. 3:7). But the same principle obviously cuts both ways. How can we expect to be at peace with God in prayer when we are sowing disunity in our own homes? Being ugly to our wives (or husbands) is a backbreaker in prayer.

8. *Praying while ignoring the poor.* Scripture is replete with the compassion of God for the poor, the needy, the helpless victim, the voiceless, and those who suffer persecution and injustice. When you show compassion to those in need, God shows favor on your requests. But the opposite is true as well. "He who shuts his ear to the cry of the poor will also cry himself and not be answered" (Prov. 21:13). If you snub the poor and destitute as if they're less than human, an eyesore—or just completely invisible—expect to feel blockage in your experience of prayer. Needy sinners like ourselves shouldn't feel more deserving of the Father's care and notice than the needy around us.

9. *Praying with bitterness in your heart toward someone.* It is sinful to receive God's forgiveness, totally undeserved, and then consider ourselves exempt from the command and responsibility of forgiving others who've offended us. "Whenever you stand praying," Jesus said, "forgive, if you have anything against anyone, so that your Father who is in

heaven will also forgive you your transgressions. But if you do not forgive, neither will your Father who is in heaven forgive your transgressions" (Mark 11:25–26). Bitterness is a toxin that not only poisons us spiritually, mentally, even physically, but also poisons the effectiveness of prayer and the full experience of our relationship with God.

10. *Praying with a faithless heart.* One final barrier to prayer is the basic prerequisite of belief. Hebrews 11:6 says, "Without faith it is impossible to please Him, for he who comes to God must believe that He is and that He is a rewarder of those who seek Him." Whenever we don't trust someone and are convinced they don't have the capability or willingness to do what they say, a breach clouds that relationship. The same thing happens when we don't believe God can help us with what we need. We should "ask in faith without any doubting, for the one who doubts is like the surf of the sea, driven and tossed by the wind. For that man ought not to expect that he will receive anything from the Lord, being a double-minded man, unstable in all his ways" (James 1:6–8). Lukewarm belief is the weakest form of praying. Doubt locks us out of our own prayer closets.

> *Lord, reveal to me anything that is hindering my prayer life, and help me get rid of it quickly. If there is any arrogance in me, pretense, manipulation, bitterness, ruthlessness, or a lack of faith in You, forgive and cleanse me, Lord. I forgive those who have wronged me as You have forgiven me. I thank You for Your kindness and patience. I'm tired of being the one who's blocking*

myself from being as close to You as possible and receiving what You desire to give me. Unhinge me, I pray, from any locks of prayer. Open me up so You can work without hindrance through me. In Jesus' name, amen.

12

HOW: THE KEYS OF PRAYER

Call to Me and I will answer you, and I will tell you great and mighty things, which you do not know. (Jer. 33:3)

While the locks of prayer lead us to repent and deal with wrong attitudes in our heart, the keys of prayer launch us forward into vibrant and effective praying. They help us live victoriously and know God in richer and fuller ways. The keys make prayer more genuine, pleasing, and authentic. Let's explore the ten keys of prayer.

1. *Praying persistently by asking, seeking, and knocking.* We're accustomed to busy people who don't have time to be interrupted. Unless, that is, the important person we're wanting to see is someone who truly loves and cares for us, which is exactly what happens in prayer. Based on this relationship—Father to child—that's why we're told to "keep asking, and it will be given to you. Keep searching, and you will find. Keep knocking, and the door will be opened to you. For everyone who asks receives, and the one who searches finds, and to the one who knocks, the door will

be opened" (Matt. 7:7–8 HCSB). One of the most astonishing keys of effective prayer is to not hold back in our asking—and to *keep* asking, persistently, day after day. He will answer when the time is right. But we will know it's Him who's giving if we haven't given up in asking.

2. *Praying in faith.* People who don't think they'll get what they pray for will likely not get what they pray for. But it's not supposed to be this way . . . God is pleased with faith. Jesus praised those who asked in faith. To fully trust Him and His Word appeals to the heart of God. Jesus said, "I say to you, all things for which you pray and ask, believe that you have received them, and they will be granted you" (Mark 11:24). Certainly we know prayer is not a magic genie lamp. But because it's based on loving relationship—the more God's Spirit communicates His will to us—we can more clearly come to know what He's wanting to give us. To know where He's wanting to take us. So we can pray with full belief that He can and will bring it to pass. That's praying in faith. And that's praying with effectiveness.

3. *Praying in secret.* Jesus said in Matthew 6:6, "But you, when you pray, go into your inner room, close your door and pray to your Father who is in secret, and your Father who sees what is done in secret will reward you." One of the bedrock principles of Christian living is that "whatever a man sows, this he will also reap. For the one who sows to his own flesh will from the flesh reap corruption, but the one who sows to the Spirit will from the Spirit reap eternal life" (Gal. 6:7–8). To pray for show is sowing to the flesh, but to pray in secret is to approach God with greater focus and humility. For He is in the secret place with us.

4. *Praying according to God's will.* Our natural tendency is to think of God's will as hidden and mysterious. However, that's not what the Bible says. By presenting ourselves to God and not being "conformed to this age," by being "transformed" with a renewed mind, we *can* "discern what is the good, pleasing, and perfect will of God" (Rom. 12:1–2 HCSB). So prayer waits on God to show us where He's ready for us to go (or not go). And once we sense it, "this is the confidence which we have before Him, that, if we ask anything according to His will, He hears us. And if we know that He hears us in whatever we ask, we know that we have the requests which we have asked from Him" (1 John 5:14–15). When we genuinely desire the knowledge of His will—and are committed to following it once we know it—He will inspire us with a new level of assurance in prayer.

5. *Praying in Jesus' name.* Those words—"in Jesus' name"—are not just the "Sincerely Yours" at the close of our prayer. Not just the "send" button. They are reflective of an unselfish, God-honoring heartbeat within ourselves. They are a statement of both worship and admitted need. They honor His power and authority while celebrating His willingness to apply them to our lives. "Whatever you ask in My name," He tells us, "that will I do, so that the Father may be glorified in the Son. If you ask Me anything in My name, I will do it" (John 14:13–14). Praying in His name means to pray as He would. To pray from within our relationship with Him. We don't approach God based on our authority, our righteousness, or what we've done, but based upon Christ's and what He's done.

6. *Praying in agreement with other believers.* To really zoom your prayer experiences off the charts, develop the regular habit of praying with other believers. Jesus told His disciples, "If two of you agree on earth about anything that they may ask, it shall be done for them by My Father who is in heaven. For where two or three have gathered together in My name, I am there in their midst" (Matt. 18:19–20). To agree means to make a harmonious symphony. Praying in unity with one another, asking for the same thing with one heart and mind, pleases God. He loves and honors the synergy that occurs when we gather with others to pray. We should pray with a ready "Yes" and "Amen" in our hearts as others pray. Approaching our Father together. Both formally and informally. Scheduled and impromptu. The power and beauty of united prayer is a gift we too often leave untouched and unopened. Who can you begin praying with? Start with the people in your family. Consider praying together often for every need.

7. *Praying while fasting.* Another overlooked key is the dedicated discipline of fasting—going without food (or some other sort of daily need) in order to focus more fully on the Lord for a concentrated period. Jesus fasted and prayed. Esther fasted and prayed. Nehemiah fasted and prayed. Acts 14:23 describes how Paul and Barnabas, in their ministry travels, would appoint elders in the various churches they were planting. Choosing the right leadership was vital. So they didn't just hold a meeting to work on their plans. They "prayed with fasting." Fasting opens up your spirit to God when you would otherwise be feeding your flesh. It clears

the air of distraction. It puts seeking Him above all your appetites.

8. *Praying from an obedient life.* "If our heart does not condemn us, we have confidence before God; and whatever we ask we receive from Him, because we keep His commandments and do the things that are pleasing in His sight" (1 John 3:21–22). An obedient child gains great favor and freedom with his or her parent. The intimacy you desire with God travels through the connective bond of your obedience to Him. When praying from an obedient heart, we can freely make requests without shame. Working *with* Him instead of working *against* Him.

9. *Praying while abiding in Christ and His Word.* Jesus said, "If you abide in Me, and My words abide in you, ask whatever you wish, and it will be done for you" (John 15:7). Abiding means staying in close fellowship with someone. It involves spending time in God's Word, allowing it to fill our hearts and guide our thinking, walking in obedience to what He tells us to do (John 15:10), receiving God's love, then pouring it back out on Him and the people around us. (John 15:9, 12). Lastly, *abiding* means staying clean before God (John 15:3; 1 John 1:9) by not allowing "ungodliness" or sin to build up or go unconfessed. It is within this context that our prayer lives are opened up into a fresh vibrancy, fruitfulness, and effectiveness before God (John 15:5). John 15:7 implies that abiding in this way opens up our prayers to also ask for good things that our hearts desire.

10. *Praying while delighting in the Lord.* When God becomes your greatest delight and first love above all else, then you are in a position for Him to bless you with your

heart's desires. Only in receiving His salvation—replacing our hostility for righteousness with the purity of His own righteousness—do we become able to truly love Him. And in loving Him, we desire to obey Him (John 14:15), until we actually begin delighting in Him. "Delight yourself in the LORD," the Bible says, "and He will give you the desires of your heart" (Ps. 37:4). The Hebrew word for "desires" is the word for petitions. When your delight is in Him and in honoring His desires, then He takes delight in you and in honoring yours.

Lord, You are a good and loving God. You didn't need to allow us to know You and pray to You, but You did. I thank You that through Jesus we can boldly approach Your throne of grace in our time of need. Make me a strong and effective prayer warrior. Help me walk closely with You, to pray in faith, in Jesus' name and in agreement with other believers. May I delight in You above all else. Give us grace and faith to trust You for great things. And prompt us with great requests so we can lift them back to You and watch You answer them for our delight and for Your glory. In Jesus' name, amen.

13

VERTICAL: THE CROSS OF CHRIST

*He Himself bore our sins in His body on the cross, so that
we might die to sin and live to righteousness. (1 Pet. 2:24)*

 The primary reason why many religious people can never seem to show much evidence of answered prayers in their lives is because they've never truly entered into a personal, saving relationship with Jesus Christ. They have religion and *know about* God, but they don't truly have a relationship and *know* Him personally.

Jesus warned, "Not everyone who says to Me, 'Lord, Lord' will enter the kingdom of heaven, but only the one who does the will of My Father in heaven. On that day many will say to Me, 'Lord, Lord, didn't we prophesy in Your name, drive out demons in Your name, and do many miracles in Your name?' Then I will announce to them, 'I never knew you! Depart from Me, you lawbreakers!'" (Matt. 7:21–23 HCSB). Admittedly, this is one of the most terrifying passages in the Bible. But Jesus is not trying to haunt us with these words. He's trying to help us.

So before diving into what all is involved in developing a more vibrant and effective prayer life, the first place for anyone to start is by pausing to make sure they've even begun a genuine relationship with God in the first place.

The apostle Paul said, "Test yourselves to see if you are in the faith; examine yourselves! Or do you not recognize this about yourselves, that Jesus Christ is in you—unless indeed you fail the test?" (2 Cor. 13:5).

If you think you're going to heaven simply because you're a good person, because you walked an aisle, because you prayed a prayer, because you were dedicated or baptized, because you joined a church and now actively serve as a volunteer, you should be very concerned. For while all of these things are honorable, none of them can save you. Notice how *you* are the only person mentioned in each of these situations, not God. The scribes and Pharisees also did things like these, but they didn't know God. That's why He repeatedly warned them they would be condemned at the final judgment despite their self-assurances that they were fine (Matt. 23:13–33).

Regardless of your denominational preferences a relationship with God must begin with repentance and faith in the cross of Jesus Christ. Yes, this may sound narrow to some. But there are significant reasons why Scripture points to Jesus alone as being God's provided Messiah to bridge the gap and redeem sinful people back into a loving relationship with a perfect God.

God is the One, not people, who establishes the righteous requirements for knowing Him, praying to Him, and spending an eternity with Him. We are foolish and prideful to think we get to decide these things for ourselves. That's like preschoolers on a playground arguing with each other about the rules, testing standards, and course requirements of their education. They don't have the understanding or authority to decide.

God alone created us, knows us, and possesses all authority in heaven and earth. His ways are much higher than our ways. So the real question is not "What do I think God should do?" but rather "What has He decided?" This includes morality, judgment, salvation, and (for our purposes) prayer. We don't tell God how we've decided to relate to Him and please Him, or how we will approach Him in prayer, or what and when prayers will be answered.

We must realize that when Jesus said, "I am the way, and the truth, and the life; no one comes to the Father but through Me" (John 14:6), He wasn't being prideful. He was being truthful. Being able to take the hand of God and the hand of man and bring them together, one would need to be heavenly and earthly, as well as, holy and human. And Jesus was.

Paul said, "For there is one God, and one mediator also between God and men, the man Christ Jesus, who gave Himself as a ransom for all" (1 Tim. 2:5–6). A mediator must be equal to both parties—which is why God needed to become flesh and personally provide the perfect sacrifice for our sin that His holy standards required. Because we could not.

The entire life of Jesus Christ sets Him apart as being uniquely from God and qualified to accomplish this task. The sixty-six books of the Bible fit perfectly together like a puzzle, and they point to Jesus as God's solution to our human spiritual condition (John 5:37–40).

The four historical accounts of Jesus' life in Matthew, Mark, Luke, and John share detailed testimonies about His birth, teachings, miracles, death, and resurrection. And the theological books of Romans through Revelation explain how God was spiritually offering us a means to salvation through Christ and why His death on the cross satisfied the holiness, justice, and wrath of God against sin, while simultaneously extending the merciful kindness, grace, and love of God to any sinner who is willing to trust Him by faith.

"He made Him who knew no sin to be sin on our behalf, so that we might become the righteousness of God in Him" (2 Cor. 5:21).

The book of Hebrews explains that Jesus Christ alone fulfilled every one of God's requirements for a Savior, including being a sinless, blood sacrifice as punishment for sin (Lev. 17:11), the fulfillment of God's law (Heb. 9:19–22), the establishment of a perfect covenant between us and God (Heb. 8:6), and an endless priesthood that could forever carry out this covenant (Heb. 7:20–28). No other religious leader comes even close to being able to do, explain, or provide what Christ has for us.

But that's all right, because Jesus also lovingly offers a salvation that is all-inclusive in its reach, meaning that anyone, anywhere can be saved (John 3:16; 1 John 2:1–3). So to say that "Christ alone" is too narrow of a truth is actually the *opposite* of the truth, because anything but Christ will not reach all, deal with the sins of all, or offer eternal life beyond the grave to "whoever will call on the name of the Lord" (Rom. 10:13).

In addition to this, salvation that comes by grace through faith separates Christianity from every other religion in the world. God offers us forgiveness and eternal life as a free gift (Rom. 6:23; Eph. 2:8–9), rather than requiring us to spend a lifetime of sacrifice trying to earn heaven and God's forgiveness through a list of seemingly impossible religious rituals. He does this to reveal His loving-kindness and great mercy and is glorified when we receive His gift by faith.

As Scripture says, "He saved us, not on the basis of deeds which we have done in righteousness, but according to His mercy, by the washing of regeneration and renewing by the Holy Spirit, whom He poured out upon us richly through Jesus Christ our Savior, so that being justified by His grace we would be made heirs according to the hope of eternal life" (Titus 3:5–7).

With this in mind, it is important to make sure we submit to God's plan and are saved God's way through Jesus, not on our own. Jesus said, "Truly, truly, I say to you, unless one is born again he cannot see the kingdom of God" (John 3:3). Salvation comes from the Lord, not man. It is a spiritual transformation God brings about within someone's heart and life. No individual or church can manufacture it. But God does it as we repent and trust Christ alone by faith.

His Word says, "If you confess with your mouth Jesus as Lord, and believe in your heart that God raised Him from the dead, you will be saved; for with the heart a person believes, resulting in righteousness, and with the mouth he confesses, resulting in salvation" (Rom. 10:9–10).

So what about you? What or who are you trusting in? Yourself, your church, your goodness, your upbringing? Or Jesus? Have you truly been born again as Jesus said must happen?

Eternity is too long to be wrong about your ultimate destiny. The book of 1 John gives us seven key salvation indicators that help a person determine if they truly know God or not. We challenge you to test yourself using the biblical guidelines that appear at the end of this chapter. When you read through them, ask if these "fruits of true salvation" are currently in your life.

If you've discovered you may not truly know God through Christ, then we invite you now to repent of your sins, repent of trusting in yourself, and place your faith now in surrender to Jesus Christ, trusting in His cross alone for salvation. (We've provided a guided prayer on page 230, if this is the desire of your heart.)

What we've just discussed is the first step in fulfilling the purpose of this book. If you've repented and trusted Jesus Christ as your Lord and Savior, this is the foundation for a strong prayer life. The Bible says God is, therefore, your heavenly Father (John 1:12), you are His beloved child (Eph. 1:5–6), His Holy Spirit has entered your heart (Eph. 1:13–14), you've been redeemed and cleansed by the blood of Jesus (Eph. 1:7), and you now have access and freedom to approach God boldly in prayer (Eph. 3:12). This is what knowing Christ does for us, not to mention opening up for us an amazing prayer communication line with God!

Beyond this, learning to grow in intimacy, faith, and closeness with God will be the next steps in building upon this foundation.

Heavenly Father, I come to You by faith in Jesus Christ, Your Son, and through His shed blood on the cross as just payment for my sins. I confess that I am a sinner and that I believe Jesus Christ died for me and rose again from the grave proving that He's the Son of God. I acknowledge my faith in You and confess Jesus now as my Lord and Savior forever. I thank You for reaching out to me in love and for providing a way for people to be forgiven and know You and spend an eternity with You. Help me live out my identity in Christ and to humbly walk in obedience and love to Your leadership and commands. Help me take full advantage of the access I've been given through Christ to approach You daily in prayer. In Jesus' name, I pray, amen.

SEVEN INDICATORS OF TRUE SALVATION

If you were put on trial for being a Christian, would the evidence of your life be overwhelmingly clear that you know Christ and that He knows you? Genuine salvation is a life-changing experience. "If anyone is in Christ, he is a new creature; the old things passed away; behold, new things have come" (2 Cor. 5:17).

Good works do not remove sins, nor can they save anyone. But after a person is genuinely saved and is truly transformed by Christ, specific good works will start showing up as evidence or proof of their salvation. These seven things are not the cause or *roots* of salvation, but they are the *fruits* of true salvation. The book of 1 John gives us seven key indicators of genuine salvation revealing that someone is truly saved and knows God.

Indicator 1: A lifestyle of obedience to God. Though Christians stumble and make mistakes, the big picture direction and habit of a true believer becomes one of submission and obedience to Christ. They will want to read and follow God's Word. The Holy Spirit in their lives bends them toward greater and greater obedience. What about you? Have you been living a lifestyle of obedience toward God? "By this we know that we have come to know Him, if we keep His commandments. The one who says, 'I have come to know Him,' and does not keep His commandments, is a liar, and the truth is not in him; but whoever keeps His word, in him the love of God has truly been perfected. By this we know that we are in Him: the one who says he abides in Him ought himself to walk in the same manner as He walked" (1 John 2:3–6).

Indicator 2: A confession of Jesus as the Christ, God's Son. First John 2:22–23 says, "Who is the liar but the one who denies that Jesus is the Christ? This is the antichrist, the one who denies the Father and the Son. Whoever denies the Son does not have the Father; the one who confesses the Son has the Father also." While cults communicate that Jesus was merely a good teacher or prophet, God's Word says He is the Christ, the sinless Son of God, and the Lord of all. Do you openly confess that Jesus Christ is God's Son, or do you believe Him to be merely a good teacher or prophet?

Indicator 3: A lifestyle of repentance of sin. Jesus said, "Unless you repent, you will all likewise perish" (Luke 13:3). Though we all stumble in many ways (James 3:2), true believers will be confessing and turning away from sin, while false believers will not. First John 3:9–10 (NIV) says, "No one who is born of God will continue to sin, because God's seed remains in him; he cannot go on sinning, because he has been born of God. This is how we know who the children of God are and who the children of the devil are: Anyone who does not do what is right is not a child of God; nor is anyone who does not love his brother."

Indicator 4: Genuine love for other believers. "We know that we have passed out of death into life, because we love the brethren. He who does not love abides in death. Everyone who hates his brother is a murderer; and you know that no murderer has eternal life abiding in him" (1 John 3:14–15). God's Spirit pours out God's love into the hearts of God's children (Rom. 5:5; Gal. 5:22). Do you have a genuine love for other believers?

Indicator 5: The discipline of God your Father. "See how great a love the Father has bestowed on us, that we would be called children of God; and such we are" (1 John 3:1). Even as a loving earthly father disciplines his children, God promises to discipline His children when they get out of line. He says this is one of the evidences of true salvation. "God deals with you as with sons; for what son is there whom his father does not discipline? But if you are without discipline, of which all have become partakers, then you are illegitimate children and not sons. . . . All discipline for the moment seems not to be joyful, but sorrowful; yet to those who have been trained by it, afterwards it yields the peaceful fruit of righteousness" (Heb. 12:7–8, 11). Have you experienced the clear discipline of your heavenly Father in your life?

Indicator 6: The presence of God's Holy Spirit. "This is how we know that he lives in us: We know it by the Spirit he gave us" (1 John 3:24 NIV). If you are a true believer, then God's Spirit is in you and will testify with your spirit that you are a child of God (Rom. 8:16). He will also convict you when you sin (John 16:8), reveal what God's Word says when you read it (John 14:26), and pour genuine love, joy, and peace in and through you toward others (Gal. 5:22). Have you been experiencing these evidences of the Holy Spirit in your life?

Indicator 7: Faith in Jesus alone for salvation (and not yourself). "He who has the Son has life; he who does not have the Son of God does not have life. I write these things to you who believe in the name of the Son of God so that you may know that you have eternal life" (1 John 5:12–13 NIV). Or as Paul said in Philippians 3:9, "Not having a righteousness of my own derived from the Law, but that which is through faith in Christ, the righteousness which comes from God on the basis of faith." Have you been trusting in Jesus alone for your salvation, or trusting yourself or your church?

These seven indicators are signs of a *changed life*—litmus tests revealing whether God has really made you a new creation or not. They don't come naturally and are impossible to fake long-term. The world, the flesh, and the devil are all against you doing these things and will push you in the opposite direction from them. But if you look at your life over the past few months from a fifty-thousand-foot view, do you see these things?

Do you see a genuine love for other believers? Or not?

Repentance of sin? Or not?

Obedience to God? Or not?

The discipline of your Father? Or not?

The evidence of God's Spirit? Or not?

A confession of Jesus as God's Son? Or not?

A genuine faith in Jesus alone for salvation? Or not?

If these indicators reveal a true relationship with Christ, then rejoice and rest in it. If they do not, then don't put off the command of Scripture to repent and believe in Jesus Christ, placing your faith in Him alone for genuine salvation. (Again, turn to page 230 for help in praying to receive Christ.)

14

Vertical: Repentance Versus Pride

Humble yourselves in the presence of the Lord,
and He will exalt you. (James 4:10)

 Jesus described two men who went to the temple to pray (Luke 18:9–14). One was an impressive, religious Pharisee and the other a sinful tax collector. The Pharisee stood and expressed thanks for what a great guy he was—unlike the wicked sinners around him. He boasted about the good things he had done and self-righteously assumed he didn't need to repent of anything. But the tax collector stood off by himself, recognized his need for God and forgiveness, lowered his head in repentance, and begged the Lord for mercy in light of his sins.

Jesus ended the story by saying the tax collector walked away justified and right with God, but the prideful Pharisee did not. This parable was likely shocking to Jesus' audience because they esteemed Pharisees as being holy before God, but viewed tax collectors as the sinful scum of the earth. Here's how Jesus drew the bottom line: "Everyone who exalts himself will be humbled, but he who humbles himself will be exalted" (v. 14).

Which attitude best describes how you approach God in prayer: humbly or pridefully? In humility we more clearly see our need for God—for His guidance, grace, and forgiveness. And in humility we honestly admit our sin and willingly cry out to Him while turning away in repentance from anything that displeases Him. Pride, however, resists this attitude—too vulnerable, beneath us, a sign of weakness. Pride assumes self-sufficiency and boasts of self-righteousness.

Pride says, "I'm a good person. I haven't done anything that bad. I don't really need to repent of anything." Pride also proclaims, "This is my life. I'm in control. I should get what I want and get the credit for what I do." In terms of our relationships with others, pride quietly whispers, "I know better than they do. I'm more important than they are. I deserve better than what they get." Basically, "Mine is the kingdom, mine is the power, and mine is the glory."

The deception behind pride is that it makes us believe we're much more important than we really are. "For if anyone thinks he is something when he is nothing, he deceives himself" (Gal. 6:3). We get into trouble anytime we overlook the fact that our lives are a gift from God and we are undeserving of the mercy, grace, and blessings He has given us. Even our accomplishments come only as a result of abilities He's given us. That's why pride is one of the greatest sins of all (Prov. 6:16–17). It leads to almost every other sin.

Proverbs 11:2 warns, "When pride comes, then comes dishonor, but with the humble is wisdom." The irony is that prideful people see themselves as wise. They are looking to gain honor believing they likely deserve it. But the opposite is true. A prideful attitude hurts us and disqualifies us, while a humble attitude is what God blesses and builds up.

Proverbs 29:23 concludes, "A man's pride will bring him low, but a humble spirit will obtain honor." The lack of humility in today's culture is in part what blinds us to our desperate need to seek God daily in prayer and to walk in repentance. It's hard to be sorry for what you're proud of and to ask for forgiveness when you don't really think you need it.

As we look at those in Scripture who walked closely with God and were used in miraculous ways, we find a consistent attitude of humility. David, Israel's greatest king, repeatedly asked, "Who am I?" feeling unworthy of the things he experienced (1 Sam. 18:18; 1 Chron. 17:16; 29:14). The apostle Paul called himself the "chief" of sinners (1 Tim. 1:15 NKJV)—the "worst of them," the "foremost of all"—yet he wrote almost half of the New Testament and was used of God to draw countless thousands to faith in Christ. In the Old Testament, Joshua bowed humbly before the Lord, recognizing his need for God's help, and God conquered the Promised Land through him. Esther walked in humility and submission, even when acting boldly for her people, and God protected the Jews from extinction. Daniel maintained a humble spirit in Babylon, gaining favor from the king.

All of us could admit that when we're around others who think too much of themselves, their attitude disgusts us. God would agree. Speaking to our relationships, God's Word says, "All of you, clothe yourselves with humility toward one another" (1 Pet. 5:5). Think about this. What would change in our marriages, homes, and church relationships if we all *clothed ourselves with humility* toward one another? We would be more others-centered and less self-centered. More thankful, less complaining. More respectful, less judgmental. More cooperative, less stubborn. Harder to offend, more readily apologizing. We would listen to advice, counsel, and rebuke rather than getting upset when confronted. Basically, we would be more like Jesus and less like Satan.

"Therefore humble yourselves under the mighty hand of God, that He may exalt you at the proper time, casting all your anxiety on Him, because He cares for you" (1 Pet. 5:6–7).

James 4:6 tells us God is opposed to the proud but gives grace to the humble, and that we should submit ourselves to God and resist the devil (who wants us to walk in pride). God tells us to draw near to Him, knowing He will then draw near to us as we repent and seek His cleansing. So why carry self-pride in our hearts? If others hate our pride and God calls it a sin, then what does it gain us? Nothing good. The things we tend to chase in life—wealth, success, applause, awards—can all lead to greater pride if obtained.

Scripture warns us, "'Let not a wise man boast of his wisdom, and let not the mighty man boast of his might, let not a rich man boast of his riches; but let him who boasts boast of this, that he understands and knows Me, that I am the LORD who exercises lovingkindness, justice and righteousness on earth; for I delight in these things,' declares the LORD" (Jer. 9:23–24).

Anything good we do or own should be redirected in service, thanksgiving, and gratefulness to God, never letting them feed any boasting or pride. Like John the Baptist, we should be looking for ways to honor Christ more and more and ourselves less and less (John 3:30). God may even lovingly send a need, weakness, or problem into our lives for a season, primarily as a real-life opportunity for learning how to walk in humility, stay close to Him, be more usable to Him, and receive more of His grace (2 Cor. 12:7–10).

To sum up, God hates pride and loves humility. It's that simple. And this truth should be branded on our hearts as we seek to walk closely with Him. The only way to properly approach a holy, sovereign, omnipotent God is in total humility and in total confession of sin. We must stay at war with our own pride, resolving to quickly deal with anything that displeases Him so we can stay unhindered in our relationship with Him and mighty in prayer. Humility is a fundamental attitude of the heart for maintaining intimacy with God and a vibrant prayer life. By repenting of our sins and humbling ourselves daily before God, we will please the Lord and pray much more frequently and much more powerfully.

Lord, too often and in too many ways I've put myself first—above my loyalty to You, above my recognition of sin, above my need for repentance, and above my humble reliance on You for everything. But where I've worked so hard to build myself up, I see now I've actually been tearing away at what my relationship with

You can be. Today, Lord, I come to You with nothing but gratitude, asking You to purge me of pride and help me see things as they really are. You first. You always.

To diagnose other areas of growth in your relationship with God, see the "Spiritual Temperature Test" on page 226.

15

HORIZONTAL: UNITY VERSUS DIVISION

Above all, put on love—the perfect bond of unity.
(Col. 3:14 HCSB)

 An interesting passage in Genesis 11 describes the construction of the tower of Babel. In this biblical account, ungodly people decided to build a city with an enormous tower for their own glory and prestige. They planned it out and began the enormous challenge, and at first found success in their efforts. But God looked down from heaven and basically said, "Because of their unity, nothing will be impossible for them." So He intervened. He divided them by changing their communication into numerous languages to prevent them from finishing their prideful monument. In their confusion and chaos, they abandoned the project and separated themselves by language, spreading out across the land.

What is so striking about this passage of Scripture is that God Himself noted that when people are unified, they are able to exert tremendous power and momentum. Even *ungodly* people! So imagine how powerful unity can be for people who worship and obey the God of the universe. If they seek the Lord and act in unity, *nothing* can stop them.

That's why the enemy does everything possible to keep God's people divided. Because once we come together in unity, we gain momentum and take ground for the kingdom.

United prayer is powerful. But prayer from a divided people . . . well, not so much. This is why removing bitterness toward others and choosing to forgive is so crucial. In fact, any pride or selfishness should be seen as an enemy of unified prayer.

In John 17, Jesus prayed a beautiful prayer, asking God to unify believers into *one body*, that the world would know He was sent by God to bring salvation to the world (v. 21). Psalm 133:1 echoes the same theme: "Behold, how good and how pleasant it is for brothers to dwell together in unity!"

God loves and blesses unity. It speaks volumes about the body of Christ when we worship together and love one another as God intended. It also draws attention to our Savior, who died to cleanse our sins and now lives to intercede for us to God the Father. When people see unity, they see purpose, love, and power. It's attractive and beautiful. And when an army of people work together to accomplish a goal, they become a formidable force indeed.

The early church in the book of Acts had this momentum. Scripture says they operated with *one mind*, devoted to prayer and to each other's needs. Their unity was so powerful and attractive, in fact, that God's hand of favor was on them, and the church grew by thousands in a brief time. Acts 2:43 says the people felt a "sense of awe" as a result.

But what do we communicate when we remain divided? When believers fuss and debate sideline issues of faith, pushing each other's hot buttons, digging into their various postures, leaving no room for anyone's way but their own way, how is the world supposed to see faith in Christ as the answer? Is Jesus divided? Or is it man's pride, selfishness, or ignorance that brings division?

Ephesians 4:1–3 (HCSB) urges us to "walk worthy of the calling you have received, with all humility and gentleness, with patience, accepting one another in love, diligently keeping the unity of the Spirit with the peace that binds us."

Powerful movements of God in the past have arisen as a result of prayer and unity. The Great Awakenings and similar revivals almost always resulted from people praying in unity, seeking God's forgiveness and cleansing, setting aside their petty differences and forgiving one another, joining hands and hearts in desperation for the Lord to show up.

And He did.

God's blessings fall when believers dwell together in unity. God moves when we rid our hearts of any sin that holds us back and seek His face together. He promises us in Mark 11:24–26 that He will grant us our needs when we forgive one another and are clean before Him. But He also warns us in 1 John 4:20–21 that we cannot hate our brother and claim to love God at the same time. When we don't forgive, then neither will He forgive us.

In order for a home to flourish, unity must dwell there, with no bitterness between husband and wife. In order for a church to flourish, unity must dwell there, with no selfish motives, bitterness, or pride. In order for a nation to flourish, unity must dwell among the people instead of a civil war of agendas, morals, and worldviews.

Romans 12:18 reminds us to live peacefully with everyone—from *our* side at least, to the extent that we can control it. But when it's beyond our influence, we pray. Fervently. Desperately. In unity with other believers. For when even two people come together in unity and truly seek the Lord, Matthew 18:20 says He is there in the midst of them.

So pray for unity. It's a powerful weapon against the enemy. Don't let him divide us over secondary issues. We must fight back by choosing to love one another, forgive one another, and seek the Lord in both humility and unity. When we do that, we gain momentum. Then when momentum builds, and when others see it, we proclaim that our unity comes because of Jesus Christ, the Son of God, who loved us and gave Himself for us.

Can you imagine churches actually working together within a city to win the lost? Can you picture pastors unselfishly praying with other pastors, sharing resources among themselves without worrying about who gets the credit? Can you see your city becoming a place where outsiders flock toward because of the powerful movement of God among a willing people? Then pray for it. Fight for it. Ask the Lord to link you with others who desire to experience it as well.

It's been done before. In the most unlikely places. And God desires to do it again. He says over and over, "Call to Me, and I will answer you, and show you great and mighty things" (Jer. 33:3 NKJV).

Oh, that God would unify us again and bring a fresh revival to our land!

Do you want it? Then what will you do?

Lord, I've seen the kind of damage that can result from being in conflict with others, when we're keeping our distance, especially among fellow believers. I've felt the hypocrisy of it all. I've kept seeing the same names and faces when convicted about people I struggle to get along with. But it's hindering me, Lord, in my prayer and in my freedom. Help me take whatever steps necessary to bring healing to any broken relationships, and to desire unity with everyone who claims the name of Christ . . . so that together we can work for Your kingdom and the glory of Your name.

16

YOUR HEART: FAITH VERSUS DOUBT

Let him ask in faith without doubting. For the doubter
is like the surging sea, driven and tossed by the wind.
That person should not expect to receive anything from
the Lord. (James 1:6–7 HCSB)

 When you pray, you should rest in the fact that God is not unaware, unable, uncaring, unwilling, or unlikely to answer. That's why He keeps prompting you to ask in faith. Your heart can be right with God and with others, and yet your doubts during prayer can create roadblocks.

Peter, for example, unnecessarily denied Jesus three times. Sometimes we, too, might quietly deny God's faithfulness, goodness, or ability in our hearts when we approach Him. This lack of faith will clog up your prayer life. You'll quit wanting to come close to God if you don't trust Him or believe He is good.

So if you don't feel like praying much anymore, the diagnosis probably lies in one of the following four misconceptions about God's heart and identity.

1. *God doesn't know or understand my needs.* Yes, He knows you. He knows you better than you know yourself. The theological word for this quality of God's nature is *omniscience*, or all-knowledge. He knows every time a sparrow falls to the ground (Matt. 10:29). He knows the number of hairs on your head (Matt. 10:30). "He counts the number of the stars; He gives names to all of them" (Ps. 147:4). "All things are open and laid bare" before His eyes (Heb. 4:13). And as we've already seen, He completely "knows what you need before you ask Him" (Matt. 6:8).

"But if He already knows what's in our heads," you might ask, "why does He want us to pray? What's the point?" Remember, prayer is about (1) intimately knowing, loving, and worshiping God; (2) conforming our lives to His will and ways; and (3) accessing and advancing His kingdom, power, and glory. All of these require interaction. God could do things without us. But He's too good and kind to kick us to the curb.

Besides, if you could possess the ability as a parent to know everything that's in your children's minds, would you prefer they ignore you? Would you want them continuing to struggle or running into trouble? Or would you rather they remained in a relationship with you so they could experience your love and wisdom in a personal way? *Of course* you'd want them close. And God does too. Yes, He does understand. And He's always here for you.

The second misconception is . . .

2. *God isn't able to help.* The apostle Paul answered this objection with one of the most resounding exclamations in the Bible, declaring that God is able not only to do whatever we can imagine Him doing, but He is "able to do *above and beyond* all that we ask or think" (Eph. 3:20 HCSB). The original Greek words that go together to form this sentence carry the idea of superabundance, exceedingly high amounts, an ability that goes beyond all forms of human measurement. That's what God has. That's who He is. Total ability and power. *Omnipotence.*

Look at the stars and look in the mirror. His creation reveals His ability to do things well. If you truly believe this, then you should have no trouble believing "if we ask anything according to His will, He hears us" (1 John 5:14). Or that with faith no larger than a "mustard seed," you can "say to this mountain"—whatever the mountain is—"'Move from here to there,' and it will move" (Matt. 17:20). Believing in such an omnipotent God means that even people like us can still be made to "stand in the presence of His glory with great joy" (Jude 24). He can truly do anything. Jesus even said, "With men this is impossible, but with God all things are possible" (Matt. 19:26). Look at His perfect track record and don't doubt His ability when you pray.

3. *God doesn't care.* The natural follow-up question, even after a person accepts God's omniscience and omnipotence, can make you ask: "If He knows everything—and can do everything—then why won't He help me? To know and not care . . . isn't that the worst quality of all?" Lack of immediate action should never be interpreted as lack of concern. Jesus pointed to the birds of the air to prove that God cares.

If He cares for them, how much more does He care for you? Every breath is a gift from Him, shouting from above that He cares.

Jesus provided two *prayer-ables* in Scripture that paint polar opposites to the caring character of God. A man gets caught off guard late at night by unexpected company. His pantry isn't stocked so he runs to a neighbor's and asks if they might spare a little bread. "Don't bother me!" comes the answer from inside. "The door is already locked, and my children and I have gone to bed. I can't get up to give you anything" (Luke 11:7 HCSB). But the man is persistent, and finally the neighbor gives him what he wants to get him to go away.

A second example is the story of a widow who was being mistreated. Bothered by the injustice, she keeps approaching a local, heartless judge to plead her case. But this official remains cold and unwilling to help. Not until she's almost worn him down by her endless pestering does he finally give in and grant her request (Luke 18:1–5).

An uncaring friend. A dismissive judge. Jesus pointed out that in both stories, the persistent requestor got what he or she asked for. His point is that God is not a calloused, uncaring judge or a sleeping neighbor in bed. Therefore, how much more quickly and willingly will He answer our requests than the judge and the sleeper? He said, "Will not God bring about justice for His elect who cry to Him day and night?" Jesus asked, rhetorically. "I tell you that He will bring about justice for them quickly" (Luke 18:7–8). So He says to us, "Ask, and it will be given you; seek, and you will find; knock, and it will be opened to you" (Luke 11:9). Not only does He care; He cares for you more than anyone else in your life. There goes another breath He just gave you.

4. *God isn't likely to do anything anyway.* That's not the impression you get from Mark 11:24—"I say to you, all things for which you pray and ask, believe that you have received them, and they will be granted you." Yes, He is willing to listen and respond and counsel and comfort and encourage and direct and rescue.

"I am willing," He said to a leper who came to Him, begging for help. He was "moved with compassion" by the faith of this broken man, and answered his prayer by healing his body (Mark 1:41). *We* are the ones who are weak and unwilling . . . unwilling to believe, unwilling to wait, unwilling to accept or have all of our questions answered. Jesus was willing to go to the cross for you. He is willing to go so far as to "save those who come to God through Him"—how?—"since He always lives to intercede for them" (Heb. 7:25 HCSB). Yes, even now, Jesus is praying and working.

As we've seen, of course, He is not a genie who grants our wishes. We should be glad of that, since we'd soon learn the horror of worshiping a God who was controlled by us, rather than one who rules all and takes all things into account. God has given us the capacity to trust that His reasons are in keeping with His wisdom and His will. Because God is sovereign, He may or may not choose to do something, even though He certainly has the ability. But whether or not He does exercise that ability, it's our job to believe He can and that He has a willing heart.

So the *Battle Plan* for your life includes the kind of praying that:

- *expects* Him to know your heart and what you truly need from Him
- *believes* that no limitations apply to Him, that He can do anything
- *anticipates* that He will respond to you with love, compassion, and mercy
- *assumes* that He is there and listening, willing to come to your aid and help you

Daily ask the Lord—in prayer—to reveal more about Himself to you as you absorb His Word, follow His teaching, apply His promises, and grow in knowledge and wisdom. Because the better you know Him, the more time you'll want to spend with Him. And the more time you spend with Him, the weaker all these misconceptions will be and the greater your faith.

And there goes another breath. He's so good.

Lord, I believe in Your perfect knowledge and understanding of me. I believe in your total, unlimited ability to accomplish Your holy will. I believe You care and are willing to help me, that I can be certain You will take the best, most loving, most appropriate actions toward me and my needs. So keep me coming to You, Lord, where all my hopes are safe and secure. And keep me asking You in faith knowing You are aware, able, caring, willing, and likely. In Jesus' name, amen.

17

YOUR HEART: SECRET
VERSUS SHOW

The secret things belong to the LORD our God.
(Deut. 29:29)

Scripture reveals that the primary way Jesus prayed was in secret. Though we have a few accounts of short prayers He prayed publicly, as well as one longer, high-priestly prayer (John 17), His routine was to either rise early to be alone in prayer (Mark 1:35), send everyone away in the afternoon and escape to a solitary place (Mark 6:46), or stay up late and pray after the others had gone to sleep (Luke 6:12).

In contrast, the religious leaders of the day were the exact opposite. Their pretentious prayer times were performances. They wanted to impress the crowds and convince everyone they were holy, spiritual giants. Jesus just called them hypocrites; in other words, actors on a stage. Consider what Jesus said in Matthew 6:5 (HCSB): "Whenever you pray, you must not be like the hypocrites, because they love to pray standing in the synagogues and on the street corners to be seen by people. I assure you: They've got their reward!"

Now let's acknowledge, everyone enjoys being loved and respected. It feels good to think those in our world think the world of us. But while being valued as a person does have some healthy benefits, our faith and service toward God should always be a matter of humility and sincerity. And it should always be aimed at our awesome God, our Audience of One—and not for the fickle and fleeting praise of mere men.

This is not to say that praying in public is wrong. Leading others in prayer is sometimes the most loving and Christlike thing you can do. Moses, Joshua, David, Solomon, even Jesus Himself prayed before large groups of people when necessary. But they were leading others to focus on God, not to impress or fish for praise. Nor were they *afraid* to pray in public—demonstrating another form of pride—out of a fear of man. Those in the first century who "loved the praise of men more than the praise of God" (John 12:43 NKJV) were afraid to publicly identify with Christ in case it brought frowns from the Pharisees.

Regardless of what we do, we should be dead to self and let pleasing God be the goal. As the apostle Paul said: "Am I now seeking the favor of men, or of God? Or am I striving to please men? If I were still trying to please men, I would not be a bond-servant of Christ" (Gal. 1:10). We must remember that God alone created us and owns us. God alone is holy, reigning supreme, and He knows us better than we know ourselves. He alone answers prayer and will judge us one day. His opinion is the only One that matters. Seeking and pleasing Him above all should be our highest priority.

This mind-set should always affect how we pray. The reverence, humility, and sincerity with which we approach God should be reflected in how we speak to Him regardless if anyone else is listening. We must check our motives and crucify any pride whenever we are praying.

Hypocrisy must go. Fear of man must go. Leading others in prayer is a serious responsibility, never meant to spotlight the person praying but to place the focus on God alone.

So while public praying with the right motives can be important and powerful in the life of believers, Jesus' statement "when you pray" implies that your default, daily prayer life should be to "go into your private room, shut your door, and pray to your Father who is in secret. And your Father who sees in secret will reward you" (Matt. 6:6 HCSB).

Whereas united, corporate prayer can be extremely powerful in the church, Jesus implies here that getting alone and praying to God in secret is fundamental and foundational. Anyone praying for show already has the only reward they will get. Whatever feeble notoriety the audience gives is the full benefit of their "performance," not the blessings or provision from God.

In fact, God hates pride. "Everyone who is proud in heart is an abomination to the Lord; Assuredly, he will not be unpunished" (Prov. 16:5). He despises the hypocrisy of those who seek their own glory while pretending to give it to Him (Prov. 8:13; Matt. 15:8).

Secret prayer puts you in a situation where you can remove distractions, focusing all your attention on adoring

God, confessing sin to Him, thanking Him for His blessings and guidance, presenting your needs and requests to Him. It helps you stay humble, be real, and seek no other reward for your time with Him other than knowing, loving, and glorifying Him more. Secret prayer helps remove selfish motives. It's just you and God. "Therefore humble yourselves under the mighty hand of God, that He may exalt you at the proper time, casting all your anxiety on Him, because He cares for you" (1 Pet. 5:6–7).

But there's also another benefit. Jesus said in Matthew 6:6 that your Father *is in* the secret place, *sees* what is done for Him in secret, and *rewards* what is done in secret. Since God says He is present in the secret place, why would we not want to meet with Him there? And who doesn't want God to reward them? To respond to their requests? If the Son of God primarily sought His Father in secret and then commanded us to do it, why wouldn't we?

Our answers to these questions expose our hearts. Because if we find ourselves praying in front of others more than in secret, we're likely chasing the approval of men. Even if we do pray in secret but go out and brag about it, our pride again is exposed. But when no eyes are on us but the Lord's, and no ears are there to hear us but His, our motives are more pure.

Your true heart is best revealed in secret. In other words, *the secret you is the real you.* It's what you think when no one knows or hears. It's what you do when no one sees. The Proverbs, speaking wisely about a person's human nature, says, "As he thinks in his heart, so is he" (Prov. 23:7 NKJV). That's why seeking God in secret is so powerful. It tests us and tells on us.

Getting alone with God is one way of saying, "I choose You above others. I want to seek and know You and hear from You more than anyone else." When we give Him our full attention—to love Him, to worship Him, to read His Word, to listen and obey Him—He is pleased and honored. Then He chooses to bless or reward us in the way He knows is best. And He does it better than we can do it, rewarding us at "the proper time." Consider these verses . . .

"He who dwells in the secret place of the Most High shall abide under the shadow of the Almighty" (Ps. 91:1 NKJV). "For in the time of trouble He shall hide me in His pavilion; in the secret place of His tabernacle He shall hide me; He shall set me high upon a rock" (Ps. 27:5 NKJV). "The secret of the Lord is with those who fear Him, and He will show them His covenant" (Ps. 25:14 NKJV).

The secret to your success will come from your secret place. And the secret to your failure will come from your failure in the secret place.

So go there. Abide there. Escape there. Worship there. Pray there.

And keep it a secret.

O Lord, show me why I pass up so many opportunities to get alone with You. Help me realize my time with You in quiet is priceless. It's where I can hear from You best, be the most honest before You, and enjoy the most blessings of Your presence and rewards. Thank You, Lord, for choosing to be so near to me, and for inviting me to spend time alone with You, just the two of us. Help me die to my pride and then delight in spending time alone with You.

18

YOUR HEART:
OBEDIENCE VERSUS
REBELLION

*Let us draw near with a sincere heart in full
assurance of faith, having our hearts sprinkled
clean from an evil conscience. (Heb. 10:22)*

Imagine telling your children to go clean their messy rooms. Two hours later you walk in and see them in a circle on the floor, holding hands, praying for God to reveal His will about whether they should begin. You hear them asking Him to give them the spirit of cleanliness, to equip them with everything needed to straighten up what's so dirty and out of order.

Lofty prayers, but no submission. Rebellion wrapped in intercession. How would you react to that? You'd likely tell them to stop the performance and get busy doing what you'd already told them to do. Praying more is clearly not what they need to be doing at the moment. *Obedience* is.

But that's how a lot of people handle prayer. They hide behind it. They hope it will cover for disobedience in other areas that are a lot harder and more costly to do than just praying. God keeps telling them to do things, but they keep "praying about it" with no steps of action.

A lifestyle of obedience—while not a condition that earns salvation—is a major key to answered prayer. If you have a child who listens and obeys you, and another who ignores you and rebels, to which child are you more likely to give what they request? Why should anyone call Jesus "Lord, Lord" if they're not serious about doing what He says? (Luke 6:46).

The logic couldn't be more clear. And Jesus couldn't have said it more plainly: "If you love Me, you will keep My commandments" (John 14:15). We're not saying we're capable of always doing things perfect, but how can we argue with His statement? To not follow Him with faith and submission while claiming total allegiance is the same as saying our love for Him is a cup of lukewarm coffee at best.

So while the idea of God telling us *not* to pray sounds counterintuitive in one sense, the fact is unavoidable: prayers generated by a rebellious heart are contradictory to one another. That's why the Bible does reveal this surprising directive on more than one occasion—telling us *not* to pray.

When Joshua, for instance, was trying to understand Israel's humiliating defeat at the small city of Ai, especially after their rousing victory at the much more heavily fortified city of Jericho, God said to him, "Rise up! Why is it that you have fallen on your face? Israel has sinned, and they have also transgressed My covenant which I commanded them" (Josh. 7:10–11). The better course of action, He said, was to go find the source of the problem, remove it from the camp, and then the relationship would be restored. Stop praying and start cleaning house.

God instructed several of the prophets to halt their prayers for a wayward generation in Israel. "Do not pray for this people, and do not lift up cry or prayer for them, and do not intercede with Me; for I do not hear you. Do you not see what they are doing in the cities of Judah and in the streets of Jerusalem?" (Jer. 7:16–17). He rhetorically asked—as long as they persisted in their idolatry—"shall I be inquired of by you, O house of Israel?" (Ezek. 20:31). "If you consent and obey, you will eat the best of the land; but if you refuse and rebel, you will be devoured by the sword" (Isa. 1:19–20).

Obedience matters. Not in a legalistic way. Not as a means of pride or comparison with others. But life as a follower of Christ was never meant to be a casual attempt at doing as little as necessary—just enough to get by, just enough to feel good about going to church on Sunday morning. A person who is truly in Christ is steadily moving in a direction of greater obedience to Him. "Everyone who has this hope fixed on Him purifies himself, just as He is pure. . . . The one who practices righteousness is righteous, just as He is righteous" (1 John 3:3, 7).

Prayer offers you the ongoing incentive to keep pursuing it. Wanting to be close to Him is worth it. The honor of being able to come to Him, praising Him, enjoying Him, on the same page with Him is an experience no "passing pleasures of sin" can ever provide (Heb. 11:25). And with each victory, with each new burst of spiritual momentum, you don't want anything of yours standing in the way between yourself and Him.

"To the faithful you show yourself faithful, to the blameless you show yourself blameless, to the pure you show yourself pure." It's the "crooked" who see God as "shrewd," as if He's someone we feel the need to wrestle against and contend with (Ps. 18:25–26 NIV). Praying with a clean heart is like driving with a clean windshield. Everything God does looks better through it.

So "beloved, if our heart does not condemn us, we have confidence before God; and whatever we ask we receive from Him, because we keep His commandments and do the things that are pleasing in His sight" (1 John 3:21–22). Are you keeping His commandments?

Look at the things you're praying for. Consider whether you're seeing them come to fruition and be clearly marked by God's blessing. If this is *not* what's happening, it doesn't necessarily mean your life is out of phase with God's Word, that you're not walking in open-hearted obedience with Him. But have you thought about checking in, just to see? To identify any holdout of rebellion or resistance in your life that He might be using this waiting time to tug out of you? Like a gardener pulling weeds, you should join Him at the root level.

Or could it be that what you're praying for is certainly coming from a willing, well-tuned heart—but what He wants from you right now isn't more prayer? He wants action. Your work orders are piling up. Is there something you've been putting off? Forgiving someone you've been trying not to think about? Keeping a promise you've been hoping they'll forget? Sometimes our prayer requests are waiting for us to travel across the bridge of faith-filled action. Is there anything God has already told you to do that you've yet to obey? Then why not start today?

Pray and obey. Obey and pray. Put those two together, and you've got a powerful combination.

Father, I pray You would forgive me for my past disobedience and rebellion—things I've never really confessed or done the hard work of forsaking. Wash me clean and turn my heart toward obeying You quickly. Today I'm going to obey Jesus Christ. I'm going to quit resisting Him and arguing with Him and rationalizing with Him and hiding behind prayer. I'm going to obey. Lord, help me obey. In Jesus' name, amen.

19

YOUR HEART: PERSISTENCE VERSUS IMPATIENCE

Indeed, none of those who wait for
You will be ashamed. (Ps. 25:3)

Persistence is a necessary part of praying effectively. Whether God answers in twenty minutes or twenty years, we should never give up on Him. In Scripture, God reveals that He wants us to trust Him patiently on our knees. He delights when we walk by faith and show our dependency on Him as we come before His throne. In fact, He may use delays in our life to reveal our hearts and our level of trust in Him. In the meantime, we must wait upon the Lord in faith.

When King Saul became impatient with God, he unwisely took matters into his own hands and paid a heavy price, losing God's blessing in the process (1 Sam. 13:8–14). But when Zechariah waited on the Lord for a child (Luke 1:5–13), he was shocked and delighted when the Angel of the Lord told him he would have a son . . . likely decades after he began praying for one.

Jesus said, "Watch therefore, and pray always" (Luke 21:36 NKJV). Paul wrote that we should "pray without ceasing" (1 Thess. 5:17) and to "continue earnestly in prayer, being vigilant in it" (Col. 4:2 NKJV). Devoted to it.

Scripture teaches this recurring lesson, time and time again, so we would catch the absolute importance of it. Jesus said in Matthew 7:7–9, "Keep asking, and it will be given to you. Keep searching, and you will find. Keep knocking, and the door will be opened to you. For everyone who asks receives, and the one who searches finds, and to the one who knocks, the door will be opened" (HCSB). He further taught in Luke 18:1 that we "ought to pray and not to lose heart."

Do you get the picture? We are not meant to pray one time for our needs or desires, and then quit or throw the prayer out the window if it's not immediately answered. God works on His timetable, not ours. But He is clearly pleased when we exercise faith and persistence because it reveals a heart that is acknowledging Him and dependent on Him.

So don't get discouraged in prayer. As in the parable of the persistent widow (mentioned in an earlier chapter)—if an ungodly, uncaring judge will respond to a persistent request, how much more will a loving, willing God respond to the persistence of His children?

The problem is never God; the problem is our lack of patience. We are so accustomed to immediate responses. We can get a fast-food meal minutes after we order it. We can get a response seconds after we text a friend. We can upload a family photo to the Internet the minute after we take it. But God is not our bellhop and doesn't owe us an immediate response. Sure, He can answer immediately if He wants, but usually He waits. For the perfect time. And His time is always gloriously better than ours.

Elijah is a good study in persistence and the various lengths of time God waited to answer prayers. When he was facing the false prophets of Baal on Mount Carmel, Elijah prayed *once*, and fire fell from heaven (1 Kings 18:37–38). When he was praying for the dead son of the widow, he prayed *three* times before the boy came back to life (17:21–22). When he was asking God to send the rain, he ended up praying *seven* times (18:41–44).

The point is, we don't know if God's answer will come immediately, after several days, or even years. But we do know He's on the throne and operates from a perfect vantage point. Sometimes He waits. And sometimes He says, "Even before they call, I will answer; while they are still speaking, I will hear" (Isa. 65:24 HCSB). He may be more glorified to wait until Abraham's a hundred years old before giving him Isaac, but God can also send Rebekah out to fetch water even before Abraham's servant finishes the "amen" of his prayer asking for God to provide Isaac with a wife (Gen. 24:15).

We spoke in a previous chapter about how George Müller, one of the greatest praying men of all time, documented fifty thousand answers to prayer in his lifetime, including five thousand answered on the same day he prayed them. But even at that astounding rate, this means ninety percent of his answers to prayer came later—sometimes *decades* later. He prayed for one man's salvation for sixty-three years and never gave up. Even at Müller's death the man had not been saved. But touched by the faithfulness of this servant of God, he prayed to receive Christ by the time of the funeral service.

George Müller once said, "I live in the spirit of prayer. I pray as I walk about, when I lie down and when I rise up. And the answers are always coming. Thousands and tens of thousands of times have my prayers been answered. When once I am persuaded that a thing is right and for the glory of God, I go on praying for it until the answer comes. George Müller never gave up!"

And like him, we must believe God can answer a prayer quickly while also acknowledging God's sovereignty, enough to know that He knows what's best for us and for His glory. Yet we are not to lose heart in seeking Him, for He blesses those who do so.

"Rest in the LORD and wait patiently for Him" (Ps. 37:7). "Wait for the LORD; be strong and let your heart take courage; yes, wait for the LORD" (Ps. 27:14). "I wait for the LORD, my soul does wait, and in His word do I hope" (Ps. 130:5). "Those who wait on the LORD shall renew their strength; they shall mount up with wings like eagles, they shall run and not be weary, they shall walk and not faint" (Isa. 40:31 NKJV).

God is very patient and will not delay responding to our prayers even one more day beyond what is right. His timing is perfect. Not just to the year or day, but to the second and minute. We can trust Him and should continue casting our cares upon Him with persistence and patience.

"As for me, I trust in You, O Lord; I say, 'You are my God.' My times are in Your hand" (Ps. 31:14–15 NKJV).

Lord, I don't wait well. But You have proven in Your Word that what seems like delay is actually evidence of Your care and love. So I ask You to help me apply the peace, trust, contentment, and perseverance that distinguish us as children of a good, heavenly Father. Where my flesh demands immediate action, may my heart accept Your answer on Your terms. I choose by faith to believe You can act in a moment, yet I also choose to wait. And to keep praying.

A PEARL OF PERSISTENCE

One of our favorite stories of persistence in prayer is about a dear lady in our church named Pearl. In 1964, Pearl gave her life to Christ at the age of thirty-five. And one of the first prayers she began praying, along with her husband, Richard, was that God would save her sister Mary, who lived in Long Island, New York. Pearl and Richard prayed for decades but saw no evidence of any change in her. Anytime they brought up the subject, Mary was highly resistant and would quickly say, "I'm not interested in that. I don't want to talk about that."

After Mary's husband died in 1994, she moved to Albany, Georgia, to be near Pearl and Richard. Five years later, Richard also passed away. But even without her prayer partner, Pearl and her Sunday school class at church continued to reach out to Mary, regularly interceding for her salvation. Yet nothing changed. She remained completely closed, always communicating that she wanted nothing to do with God.

Eight more years passed. In October 2007, Mary was diagnosed with Alzheimer's at ninety-one years of age. She suffered multiple strokes and started fading away mentally. By March of the next year, doctors advised she be placed under hospice care. Pearl stayed with her every day. And continued to pray.

In April, Mary stopped eating. She became dehydrated. And one day, with her body showing all signs of shutting down, she was taken to the emergency room. That night, Pearl prayed with more passion than ever—"Lord, be merciful"—begging God for her sister's salvation. She called church members, asking them to join her in prayer, sharing how she couldn't stand to see her sister die without Christ.

But Mary's body could fight no longer. Around 10:00 p.m., her heart stopped beating. She died in her bed, right there in the emergency room, still having never trusted Christ.

It was over. Or was it?

An alarm went off in her room. Doctors rushed back in. Despite the previous confirmation that her heart had stopped, they gave her a shot, shocked her system, and revived her. Pearl started to wonder: maybe God wasn't finished with Mary even yet.

Meanwhile, the senior adult minister at our church—a man named Tom—was lying in bed trying to go to sleep, when he felt as though God was telling him something. He had gotten to know Mary through the years, as a result of his interactions with Pearl. And he knew, of course, through his role with the senior adults, all about Mary's physical condition, including the fact that she'd been taken to the hospital that day. Although it was late, although he was tired, he allowed the restless urging in his spirit to prevail. He and his wife, Pat, got up, changed clothes, drove to the hospital, and walked into the room where Mary was being cared for.

She was unusually awake and coherent when they arrived, especially in light of her brush with death in the last few hours. She recognized Tom immediately, greeting him with the words, "Tom, I kicked the bucket today." He took her by the hand, saying, "Mary, you know it's the late hour. God is still willing to save you. Don't you think it's time you gave your life to Jesus Christ?"

What could she say? She said yes. She was ready now to do that. She prayed with Tom and gave her life to Christ in the emergency room . . . to the indescribable joy of her patient, prayerful sister.

Mary remained very ill, however. A few days later, she died. But the hospice workers, who'd always noticed the sad, tired look on her face, said they'd never seen anyone with a more peaceful expression as she passed away.

This story was a huge encouragement for the people in our church. The church family heard the good news and rejoiced over God's faithfulness to answer prayer. Pearl still reminds people to never give up in prayer. "We just cannot give up or stop," she says.

20

THE WORD OF GOD

The commandment of the LORD is pure,
enlightening the eyes. (Ps. 19:8)

If your heart is right with God and others and you are ready to pray, then what should guide your praying? True, prayer can flow directly from your heart. No script is necessary. Nothing prescribed or recited. Prayer is personal. Completely unique. Yet even with this much freedom involved, God does provide powerful resources to help us pray strategically and specifically. To help you know for certain that your heart is beating in step with God's.

Perhaps the first and most comprehensive guide of all is to pray to God using the very words He's already spoken in His Word.

We humans are fickle. Hot and cold. Moods and emotions that flame within us today can be nearly forgotten memories by the end of the week. But when we pray with words and thoughts that are inspired by Scripture, we're assured that our praying is anchored in bedrock truths that stretch back centuries, millennia, even into eternity. They keep our praying steadfast and consistent.

You may think, "Well, I don't know the Bible well enough. I wouldn't know where to look for passages that talk about things relevant to me." But that's not a problem. You can pray about that too. God will guide you as you seek Him. Because what you find as you begin devoting yourself to reading, studying, and meditating on the Word is that the Holy Spirit quickly begins causing Scripture to be "implanted" in your heart (James 1:21). Jesus tells you to "abide" in Him and let His words "abide" in you. Those are the conditions through which you can "ask whatever you wish, and it will be done for you" (John 15:7). So you'll be surprised, not only by how often He'll bring a verse to mind as you're praying, but by how many verses, from so many different places, He can bring to apply to your need at a given moment. The more you abide in the Word—reading it, journaling it, underlining it, memorizing it—the more it will become second nature, almost like a second language.

Perhaps you and your friends or family are fans of a certain movie or television show. You've watched it so many times that occasionally you'll answer one another with a line from one of the characters. It's become part of your shared vocabulary.

The same principle applies with Scripture—only better—because the Bible is not composed of stale, dated, inanimate words. The Bible is alive and active. Henry Blackaby, author of *Experiencing God*, has long instructed believers not to refer to the Bible as what "*it* says" but what "*He* says"— what *God* says. Unlike every other book you've ever read, the Writer of the words lying open in front of you is right there in the room with you. He is here. He is speaking. And perhaps best of all, He is listening.

So like Paul said, when you take up "the sword of the Spirit, which is the word of God," putting on your spiritual armor, you can use this Word to "pray at all times in the Spirit" (Eph. 6:17–18), communicating with the Lord based on His living communication with us.

Nehemiah's prayer in the Old Testament, when he heard about the desperate, dilapidated conditions in Jerusalem during the exile, is an example of this prayer strategy. The disturbing news from his homeland broke his heart, and he prayed for days that God would bring restored strength and recovery to the people who were living there or return-ing there. He confessed in his prayer that Israel had sinned against the Lord. He understood (from Scripture) that they were deserving of what they'd suffered. For like God had said to the people ages before through Moses, "If you are unfaithful I will scatter you among the peoples" (Neh. 1:8). But Nehemiah remembered, too, something else God had said: "If you return to Me and carefully observe My com-mands, even though your exiles were banished to the ends of the earth, I will gather them from there and bring them to the place where I chose to have My name dwell" (v. 9 HCSB). Nehemiah was able to pray with confident hope and promise because he knew how God's nature applied to times like these.

And you can do the same thing. When feeling fatigued, you can pray knowing that "those who trust in the LORD will renew their strength; they will soar on wings like eagles;

they will run and not grow weary; they will walk and not faint" (Isa. 40:31 HCSB).

When stressed and outmatched by a particularly arduous challenge, cry out to Him "from the end of the earth," like David did, saying, "when my heart is overwhelmed; lead me to the rock that is higher than I" (Ps. 61:2 NKJV). Three thousand years later, God is still there to be called upon.

When unsure what to do next, perhaps doubting for a moment that He either cares or is able to help, remind yourself in prayer that "those who know Your name will put their trust in You, for You, O LORD, have not forsaken those who seek You" (Ps. 9:10).

King David worshiped, as you can worship, by saying to the Lord, "You satisfy me as with rich food; my mouth will praise You with joyful lips" (Ps. 63:5 HCSB). Before going to bed at night, he looked into God's face as his last thought of the day, saying, "When I awake, I will be satisfied with Your presence" (Ps. 17:15 HCSB). He wanted God to be his first thought and first prayer in the morning as well.

The Word can guide your prayers of *adoration:* "Yours, O LORD is the greatness and the power and the glory and the victory and the majesty. . . . You rule over all, and in Your hand is power and might" (1 Chron. 29:11–12).

Your prayers of *confession:* "Create in me a clean heart, O God, and renew a steadfast spirit within me. . . . Restore to me the joy of Your salvation and sustain me with a willing spirit" (Ps. 51:10, 12).

Your prayers of *thanksgiving:* "Give thanks to the LORD, for He is good; for His lovingkindness is everlasting. . . . I shall give thanks to You, for You have answered me, and You have become my salvation" (Ps. 118:1, 21).

Your prayers of *supplication:* "O LORD God of hosts, hear my prayer. . . . No good thing does He withhold from those who walk uprightly" (Ps. 84:8, 11).

The Psalms, as you can tell, are a great place to start and a rich treasury of prayers and praises. But expect the Lord to illuminate His thoughts toward you from one end of the Bible to the other. Instead of just viewing it as reading material, open your heart to receive it also as prayer material. Your copy of the Bible is not only your *companion* when you enter your prayer closet; it's also your inspiration, your source, your reliable storehouse and gold mine of trustworthy promises. When you don't know what to say, let the Bible lead your praying for you.

Thank You, Lord, for Your Word. Thank You for not leaving me here to guess what You're like or what You've promised to do. I pray You'd not only fashion Your Word in my mind, but also use it to direct my hands and feet to serve You, obey You, and stay clean-hearted before You. May I truly love Your Word and cling to it as my lifeline to Your truth, love, and wisdom.

21

THE WILL OF GOD

I have come down from heaven, not to do My own
will, but the will of Him who sent me. (John 6:38)

"This is the confidence which we have before Him, that, if we ask anything according to His will, He hears us. And if we know that He hears us in whatever we ask, we know that we have the requests which we have asked from Him" (1 John 5:14–15).

The best place in the world for any of us to be is squarely in the middle of God's will. It is His perfect plan that will bring Him the most pleasure. It is not only what's best for us, but it's what will yield God the most glory. And thankfully, He has promised every one of His children that we can live in His will continually.

Many people are convinced that God's will is a mystery. Unknowable. All shadows and secrets. Best hunches and wild guesses. And sometimes, when trying to discern His will for a major decision, the predominant feeling at first can be indecision. Yet the best strategy to use first of all in beginning to seek God's will for specific questions is to pray like Jesus did—to pray in surrender to it from the onset.

"Not my will, but Yours be done." The presentation of our-selves can lead to the revelation of His will (Rom. 12:1–2).

Second, we should pray in accordance with what we already know for sure to be His will.

The chief goal of God's will is that He be glorified. In all circumstances. The primary driver behind all of life is that "God may be glorified through Jesus Christ" in everything (1 Pet. 4:11). "Not to us, O LORD, not to us, but to Your name give glory" (Ps. 115:1). If your desire is for the glory of God to be elevated and made known, be assured His will is going to be accomplished in you.

God's will is to advance His kingdom. In every realm. The kingdom of God is His real yet unseen rule over all creation. He is establishing His dominion on earth, even as it's already established in heaven. That's what Jesus meant by telling His followers to "seek first the kingdom of God and His righteousness" (Matt. 6:33 HCSB). As you align your goals with His kingdom goals, He promises to provide everything needed for your life to flourish.

God's will is for Christ to be Lord. In every arena. Lordship equates to power and authority. You're familiar, of course, with people who exercise power and authority over you—your boss, your leaders, police officers, parents. You do what they tell you to do. So as you follow Christ as Lord, you're saying with your life (not just your words) that you intend to give Him your full allegiance. This devoting of yourself to Him is "good and profitable for everyone" (Titus 3:8 HCSB). It's the blessing of doing His will.

Glory. Kingdom. Lordship. Those are just three major components of His overall will for you. He also wants you living a pure, sanctified life (1 Thess. 4:3). He wants you rejoicing, praying, and grateful in all circumstances (1 Thess. 5:16–18). He wants you maturing in the faith (Heb. 6:1). He wants you producing fruit, season after season (John 15:16). He wants you in close fellowship with other believers, "being of the same mind, maintaining the same love, united in spirit, intent on one purpose" (Phil. 2:2). Much of His will, therefore, is *readily* known. Not only does His Word declare it, but the Spirit affirms it in your mind and heart.

So your quest for God's will on a specific issue—whether to make an offer on this house or that one; whether to go to the smaller church nearby or the larger one across town; whether to apply for another job opportunity or stay where you are—is not really a separate matter from these other elements of His will. They're all tied together. Your knowledge on how to make a left-or-right decision, one that doesn't come with a specific Bible verse attached, will come clear in His timing as you stay focused in prayer on submitting to *all* of His will. The heart that's not only praying for His will but is also surrendering to it simultaneously—whatever the Lord reveals His plan to be—will not miss His desires when all is said and done. Because He will bail you out if you take a wrong turn (Prov. 16:9).

One of the ways God often steers us toward specific directions is by opening and closing doors of opportunity—which we're able to recognize if we're prayerfully following Him and watching for them (Rev. 3:8).

Paul often spoke of the open and closed doors God placed before him as he made decisions on where to travel next when he was planting and encouraging the early churches. Paul sometimes reported that the sense of warning over some cities was so strong, he felt "prevented" by the Holy Spirit from going there (Acts 16:6). A closed door. He spoke of other times, however, when God confirmed directions by giving him an open door to deliver the message of the gospel (2 Cor. 2:12). Once in Ephesus, the "wide door" God had unlocked for Paul's work in this region caused him to feel led to stay beyond the time he'd originally planned. And yet along with this expanded opportunity came the observation that "many oppose me" (1 Cor. 16:9 HCSB). Some might question if a hard road is truly God's will. It very well may be.

The leadership that God gives as you pray your way through hard decisions is not to be evaluated merely by the physical events happening around you. Just because His calling is seeming to lead you toward opposition or difficulty is not the cut-and-dried definition of a closed door. Sometimes the most difficult, painful, fearful, or illogical path is the one that ends up being the *open* door, the one bearing His fingerprints. When Jesus prayed, "Not My will, but Yours be done" (Luke 22:42) in the garden, He stood up to take the difficult path which was in the center of God's will.

So how do you know? What are you supposed to be looking for?

One answer is *peace* in the midst of the storm. When you're doing what you know to be the will of God—when your desire is shifted toward His *glory*, when your goal is to participate in His *kingdom*, when your impatience is swallowed up in surrendering to His *lordship*—you'll begin to "recognize His voice" above all other internal and external opinion (John 10:4 HCSB). The Holy Spirit within you, who is continually interceding for you "according to the will of God" (Rom. 8:27), will help you understand and accept what your physical eyes may not be able to see. You'll know you're staring at an opened or closed door because it will not be in contradiction to His Word and you'll be sensing His loving *peace*.

"Let the peace of Christ rule in your hearts," the Bible says (Col. 3:15). When you make known your sincere requests to Him in prayer, "the peace of God, which surpasses every thought, will guard your hearts and minds in Christ Jesus" (Phil. 4:7 HCSB).

This is not just an emotional peace that shows up for a few hours and then morphs into panic and confusion by nightfall. This distinctive "peace of Christ" settles in and is often confirmed by other believers. The enemy may try to agitate you into doubting it. But your reverent, trusting, prayerful spirit will keep Christ's peace from floating too far. You'll be able to stand before a day of unknowns, seeing the doors open and close while you calmly, peacefully wait, watch, and work. You'll discover yourself praying, "Lord, what would please and honor You most in this situation?" "Help me recognize Your desire and heart." "From what You've shown me about Yourself, how would You lead me to pray here?"

That's faith. That's obedience. That's where His will for you shines and bears fruit. And that's the kind of praying that leads remarkably to peace.

Lord, I know I'm in skillful hands as I pray for You to show me Your will and lead me faithfully into it. I accept from You specific guidance through Your Word to give me "a lamp to my feet and a light to my path" (Ps. 119:105)—for this moment. Thank You for being heaven-and-earth beyond me in size and scope (Isa. 55:8–9), yet somehow stooping down to involve Yourself in my details. Tune my heart to the desires of Your heart. Align my mind with Your thoughts. Guide my path to the center of Your plans. And help me pray and live in accordance with Your will. I love You, and I will follow You. In Jesus' name, amen.

22

THE "WHATEVER" FROM GOD

If you abide in me, and My words abide in you, ask whatever you wish, and it will be done for you. (John 15:7)

O What if the Bible said we could ask God for whatever we want, not just for what we need?

Sounds like it does, doesn't it? Did you read the words of Jesus in the above verse? Do you hear Him giving you complete permission to "ask whatever you wish?" Could that really be possible? God would actually do that for us?

Some people claim that God allows us to only ask for what we need, but never what we want. Sounds dutiful and honorable, but it's actually not biblical. The truth is, this "whatever" offer runs throughout the New Testament. It's not just an isolated statement. "Whatever you ask in prayer, believe that you have received it" (Mark 11:24). "Whatever you ask in My name, that will I do" (John 14:13). "Whatever we ask we receive from Him" (1 John 3:22). "If we know that He hears us in whatever we ask, we know that we have the requests which we have asked from Him" (1 John 5:15). There's a noticeable pattern here. A "whatever" pattern.

Now we know, of course, God is not Santa Claus. He's "established His throne in the heavens, and His sovereignty rules over all" (Ps. 103:19). And we know He will not answer requests born in sin or for sinful things (James 4:3). Yet something in His nature and in the kind of relationship He's made possible with us creates an open-door atmosphere to ask for good things. Our "whatever" requests can be met by a favorable response from Him. Otherwise, He'd never make such an audacious claim. Why would He need to?

The key is, if you are walking with Him on the path He wants you to walk, and if He's your first love, and if your heart's desire is to please Him, then He *delights* in granting your heart's desires. Your good ones. When your motivation for wanting His blessing isn't to go chasing after sin with it, but rather to find your joy in the only place where true, lasting joy can be found, the possibility of receiving your best "whatever" wishes opens up for you. With stunning regularity.

And why shouldn't it? Why should God stop giving to His children at a point where even we ourselves wouldn't stop giving to our own kids? We are not more kind than He is. We obviously don't think twice about giving our children what they really need when they ask for it. *Neither does God*. And if they ask for something we'd already planned on giving them—similar to when we ask God for something according to His will—we don't suddenly decide not to give it at the last minute. *Neither does God*. But what if they ask for something they don't technically need, but it's something good that would bring them great joy and show them our love if they had it? And what if we knew that they were consistently desiring to honor and love us and respect our rightful leadership in their lives? Would we take extra steps to try giving them their heart's desires . . . if there was any way? And yet we think God *wouldn't*?

Hannah didn't need a son, but she asked for one and God gave her one (1 Sam. 1:27). Jesus didn't need to curse the fig bush, but that was what He wanted at the time and so it happened (Matt. 21:19). Yet some people make it sound wrong to do so. They describe God like He's an impoverished, distant dad who only lets his kids ask for socks and underwear for Christmas.

When our delight is in Him—when the beat of our hearts is to say, "Lord, what can I do for You today, my Father?"—the beat of His kind heart is to say, "Well, what can I do for *you*, my child?"

Jesus declared with His mouth and demonstrated with His life that He always does what is pleasing to the Father (John 8:29). So we shouldn't be surprised hearing His friend Martha notice, "I know that whatever You ask of God, God will give You" (John 11:22). Jesus told Peter, while rebuking him for attacking the men who'd come to arrest Him, "Do you think that I cannot appeal to My Father, and He will at once put at My disposal more than twelve legions of angels?" (Matt. 26:53). That's the understood relationship between them. The Son lives to honor the Father; the Father delights in blessing the Son. And that's where each of us can live too.

When we delight ourselves in the Lord, He says He'll give us the desires of our heart (Ps. 37:4).

But that word for "desires" in the original language is actually the word *petitions*. And that's where "whatever you wish" becomes not just a pleasant thought but a powerful prayer strategy. James 4:2, as we've mentioned, tells us that one of the reasons we don't have what we want from God is because we haven't asked for it—whether through a lack of faith, an inflated trust in our own self-reliance, or other misguided reasons. But in all these "whatever" verses from the Bible, God is telling us not just to throw out these good, legitimate desires in our hearts, afraid we'd be asking too much to actually ask for them. No, ask! Turn those desires into petitions! Hit the ball into His court and see what He does with them!

Boaz so delighted in Ruth that he gave her a blank check: "I will do for you whatever you ask, for all my people in the city know that you are a woman of excellence" (Ruth 3:11).

But her request was an honorable one. Lots of people wouldn't know how to handle a blank check like this. When King Herod said to his stepdaughter Salome, "Whatever you ask of me, I will give it to you; up to half of my kingdom," (Mark 6:23), she and her wicked mother asked for the head of John the Baptist on a platter. When Samson, in his careless and sinful days, still felt like he could do whatever he wanted, he demanded a certain Philistine woman for his wife (Judg. 14:2). But he would later regret his foolish, self-gratifying demand. What we want today, we might not tomorrow. Most of the junk at garage sales is comprised of items that once seemed like something a person wanted really badly. So we should be wise and careful in the asking.

But God wants you experiencing His answers to desires that don't grow old or out of style. Like when He said to Solomon, soon after this son of David had risen to his father's throne, "Ask what you wish Me to give you" (1 Kings 3:5). The young king's request, you probably recall, was for wisdom—which the Bible says was "pleasing in the sight of the Lord that Solomon had asked this thing" (v. 10). Wisdom was what God wanted for him, too, more than wealth and long life and victory over his enemies. And because Solomon's heart was turned toward making the best choice—the one in line with the heart of God—the Lord said, "I have also given you what you have not asked, both riches and honor, so that there will not be any among the kings like you all your days" (v. 13).

How many of your desires are the kind that please the Lord when He hears them? And how might He likely respond to them if He found them so delightful?

We serve a God who "richly supplies us with all things to enjoy" (1 Tim. 6:17). He delights in His amazing creation and wants us to fully delight in Him and all the good things He's made. Think about it: He not only made food necessary and nutritious, but delightful and delicious. He could've easily made everything taste like rotten eggs and dirt. Or given us no taste buds at all. He not only made the universe functional, but also beautiful. And then He gave each of us eyes equipped with 3D, high definition, automatic focus and self-cleaning lenses that can see a billion-plus colors in panoramic real time, positioned on a pan-and-tilt, image stabilizing neck.

He could've made our seeing and hearing painful to our bodies, with every second of sight data taking months for us to mentally process. Instead He made it instantaneous and effortless. Our God makes daily sunsets beautiful, music amazingly emotional, and marital intimacy euphoric. He didn't create strawberries and honeycombs and then expect us to only have an appetite for turnips and asparagus.

The devil wants us to view God as dull and to view sin as delightful. Righteousness unpleasant and immorality liberating. But the truth is, the devil has never created anything good. Or created anything at all, for that matter. Every good and perfect gift you've ever enjoyed in life has come to you from God (James 1:17).

And because of answered prayer, you haven't seen the last of these gifts. Not if your delight is in the Lord.

Set your heart upon Him. Live to please Him. Acknowledge Him as being everything in your world. Then you're free to ask Him for the moon, knowing He'll give you either *that* wish or something even greater . . . because He delights to give His beloved children the desires of their hearts.

Lord, I'm so grateful that You delight in blessing me. And I don't want to miss a single one of them. Keep me so close to You, Lord, that nothing can stand between us. I realize no joy exists anyway outside of Your will for me, outside of the desires You've placed within me for following hard after You. I know I'll never reach the bottom of Your goodness and compassion toward me, and this truth makes me love You from the bottom of my heart.

23

THE WONDER OF
GOD'S NAMES

*O may Your glorious name be blessed and exalted
above all blessing and praise! (Neh. 9:5)*

Dr. John Smith is called different names at different times. His father calls him "Son"; his wife calls him "Sweetheart"; his patients call him "Doc"; and his friends at church call him "Brother Jack." At the hospital he's "the doctor with the best bedside manner," and the waiters at a local restaurant refer to him as "that happy Christian who leaves good tips." John isn't multiple people. He's one man with multiple roles and character traits. Each of John's names or titles reveals a little more about who he is, what he does, and how he relates to others. In like manner, the Bible reveals that our one God has many names. When we pray to Him, we may come to Him for a wide variety of reasons. Because He is eternal and limitless, the many titles and descriptions used of Him in the Bible are vast and astounding. But that's the point. Each name of God helps us to understand, value, and worship Him even more.

Unlike the Egyptians and Greeks who prayed to different mythical gods depending upon their need, we worship one God who alone is Living and Limitless, Maker and Master, Holy and Most High, Savior and Sovereign of all, and everything we need in all circumstances.

As we discover and get familiar with different names of God, we not only better recognize God for who He is, but we can relate to Him more personally and intimately.

In the back of this book is a list of many of God's names. We encourage you to learn as many as you can and to use them in your prayer times as you seek to know and worship the Lord more deeply. But for this chapter, we'll refer to a few of His names as we learn the importance of incorporating them into our prayer strategies.

As we look at Scripture, we discover that God's names reflect "His invisible attributes, His eternal power and divine nature" (Rom. 1:20). In other words, as His name is, so is He.

What an honor to discover more about God! His names are priceless to Him, a privilege for us to know, and powerful for us to pray. We are constantly referring to God's names in our interaction with Him. We call upon the name of the Lord to be saved (Rom. 10:13), proclaim the name of the Lord in our witnessing (Acts 9:20), praise the name of the Lord in our worship (Ps. 135:1), trust the name of the Lord in our daily living (Ps. 33:21), and pray in the name of the Lord in our intercession (John 14:13).

Some of God's names describe who He is, independent of what He does or what He's created: *Elohim* (God), *Yahweh*

(Lord, Jehovah), *El Elyon* (The Most High God), *El Olam* (The Everlasting God).

Some names are tied to an action He does for us: "God who avenges me" (Ps. 18:47 NKJV), the "Lord who heals you" (Exod. 15:26 NKJV), the "one who sustains me" (Ps. 54:4 NIV).

Some of His titles, positions of authority, and roles in relationship with His creation include names like: Lord, Creator, Provider, Sustainer, Almighty, Owner, and Master. The name "Elohim" (God) is the first name of God used in the Bible. It is plural and sometimes can refer to all the members of the Trinity, revealing to us that the Father, Son, and Holy Spirit were all present and part of creating the universe (Gen. 1:2, 26; John 1:1–2; Col. 1:16).

But some names refer to a specific person of the Trinity:

God the Father is sometimes called: God (Ps. 22:1; Isa. 53:4), Lord (Isa. 53:10), God and Father of Jesus Christ (1 Pet. 1:3), Father of the fatherless (Ps. 68:5), and many more.

God the Son is called: the Anointed One (Acts 4:26), the Lamb of God (John 1:29), the Christ of God (Luke 9:20), the only begotten Son (John 3:16), Alpha and Omega (Rev. 1:8), the Son of Man (John 5:27), the Author and Perfecter of our faith (Heb.12:2), King of kings, Lord of lords (Rev. 19:16).

God the Spirit is called: the Spirit of Christ (1 Peter 1:11), Counselor (John 14:16), the Spirit of the living God (2 Cor. 3:3).

God wants us to know His names so we can know Him better. They are another way we worship and praise Him—by recalling a name for Him that specifically reflects an attribute we want to honor or call upon to help address a specific need. His names are hallowed, holy, honored, and higher than every other name. That's why we must never take any of God's names in vain or use them flippantly. Rather, we praise and worship Him and His name while honoring His attributes, power, and position.

Psalm 91:1–2 describes God by saying, "He who dwells in the secret place of the Most High shall abide under the shadow of the Almighty. I will say of the LORD, 'He is my refuge and my fortress; My God, in Him I will trust'" (NKJV). In these two verses, the same God is referred to by multiple names and descriptions: *Elyon* (the Most High), *Shaddai* (the Almighty), *Yahweh* (the LORD), *my refuge, my fortress, and my God* (Elohim).

But the name of Jesus is most precious to us because "God highly exalted Him, and bestowed on Him the name which is above every name, so that at the name of *Jesus* every knee will bow, of those who are in heaven and on earth and under the earth, and that every tongue will confess that Jesus Christ is Lord, to the glory of God the Father (Phil. 2:9–11).

When we call upon Jesus Christ as our Lord, the other names of God take on infinitely more value to us. Jesus then becomes our Savior, King, and High Priest. God the Father becomes our heavenly Father and Almighty God. The Holy Spirit becomes our Helper and Counselor.

When we pray to God, we too can address Him according to who He is and what He's done, and lean on our understanding of His unending power and glory. Jesus modeled for us how to pray based upon His unique identity in the situation, like when He said, "The harvest is abundant, but the workers are few. Therefore, pray to the Lord of the harvest to send out workers into His harvest" (Matt. 9:37–38 HCSB).

Paul wrote, "Now may the God of hope fill you with all joy and peace in believing, so that you will abound in hope" (Rom. 15:13), and "May the Lord of peace Himself continually grant you peace in every circumstance" (2 Thess. 3:16).

At the same time, even without knowing a specific name, we can praise the Lord in our circumstances and declare His lordship over the need of the moment. "God, I know You are Lord over the weather, so I pray for you to send rain to our city," or "Lord, you are the Great Physician, and I ask you to guide the doctors during this surgery."

He also has more formal names. In our time of need, God is *Jehovah Jireh*—the Lord our Provider. When we struggle with sickness, He is *Jehovah Rapha*—the Lord our Healer. When we need comfort, He is *Jehovah Raah*—the Lord our Shepherd. When we are fearful or stressed, He is *Jehovah Shalom*—the Lord our Peace. And when we need to be forgiven and cleansed, He is *Jehovah Tsidkenu*—the Lord our Righteousness.

Even if you don't remember these formal names, you can praise Him in your native language by calling out to Him as the God of love, faithfulness, mercy, comfort, protection, justice, forgiveness, power, and salvation. The list goes on and on.

The point is to seek Him, worship Him, and pray to Him for who He is. To acknowledge Him as the Creator, Your Father, and the One who is everything you need. His love for you is great, and your love for Him is reflected by your desire to know Him and obey Him.

So as you pray strategically, remember to call out to your God by His names as you learn them. He loves to hear His children acknowledge Him for all He does and all He can do. And doesn't He deserve it? After all, He is God our Salvation. "Let them praise the name of the Lord: for his name alone is excellent; his glory is above the earth and heaven" (Ps. 148:13 KJV).

And to that, we say, "Blessed be the name of the LORD!"

Lord, Your name is great, just as You are great. And while You are one God—Creator of all, without rival—I praise You that You are more than I realize and everything I need. Thank You for allowing us to call on You at all times, in all circumstances, and for promising to be our All in All at every moment. I worship You today, Lord God, my Savior, my Sustainer, my Friend, my reason for living.

24

THE WISDOM OF GOD

If any of you lacks wisdom, let him ask of God,
who gives to all generously and without reproach,
and it will be given to him. (James 1:5)

 "Wisdom is supreme—so get wisdom. And whatever else you get, get understanding" (Prov. 4:7 HCSB). Not many things in life come with this kind of endorsement. *Whatever else you get. Whatever else you do.* Yet anytime we hear this kind of ultimatum, we know something important is about to be said. And when God is the One who's making the proclamation through His Word, you can be sure His advice is worth heeding.

Acquiring wisdom, He says, is of "supreme" importance. And prayer is one of the keys that unlocks it. In fact, prayer yields wisdom, and then wisdom yields better prayer.

Wisdom is the ability to apply knowledge to a given situation. Making the best choices with the data you have. To take what you know and make it work really well. To make your relationships work. To make your money work. To make grand-slam, home-run decisions about friendship, marriage, and parenting. Wisdom helps the secrets of the whiz to take root in the hearts of the dumb. It guides you to do the ethically right thing in the morally right way. It unlocks everything—things that used to seem like a mystery. When faced with dilemmas that once sent you swerving out of control, wisdom helps you locate the straight, sure path, so that "when you walk, your steps will not be hindered; when you run, you will not stumble" (Prov. 4:12). You'll be able to look back on vital moments of decision and see that you were protected from rashness and folly.

Wisdom is what we need. It helps you see things from God's eternal perspective, understand the cause and effect of a decision, and constantly learn from any situation. And God, knowing this, promises to give wisdom to those who "ask" Him for it. That word in James 1:5 not only carries the idea of asking, but of begging, calling out for something, craving it. God promises to give wisdom "generously"—especially to those who "seek [it] like silver and search for [it] like hidden treasure" (Prov. 2:4). We should want it, and want it badly.

He also says He'll give it "without reproach"—without insult or condescension. Without making fun of us for being so foolish up till now. He wants us to win. He wants to give us what we need for being successful in our families, in our work, in everything we do—"bearing fruit in every good work and increasing in the knowledge of God" (Col. 1:10). Because this gives Him glory. As much as He's glorified through our spoken praise and worship, He is glorified also through our integrity, our honesty, our diligence, our humility, our purity, our faithfulness. He is glorified by our being good spouses, parents, employees, and stewards of our resources.

King Solomon, as we saw in a recent chapter, sought the Lord for wisdom. When invited by God to ask for anything he wanted—"What should I give you?" the Lord said (1 Kings 3:5)—Solomon responded with a heartfelt request for wisdom. He was only a young man, recently ascended to his father David's throne. He admittedly had little to no experience in leadership. So he prayed, "Give Your servant an obedient heart to judge Your people and to discern between good and evil. For who is able to judge this great people of Yours?" (v. 9). God was pleased with Solomon's request, and grew him into a man whose wisdom was known far and wide. Not only did his wisdom make him known for his writing of memorable proverbs—3,000 of them, the Bible says—but also provided him the secrets of riches and honor.

One of the ways God has already answered any prayer for wisdom is with the biblical book of Proverbs—a huge collection of mostly short-answer sayings on the whole gamut of life, as seen from the perspective of both wisdom and foolishness. Polar opposites. Verifiable differences. Every time you learn a new proverb, it's like taking a giant smart pill or anti-idiot medicine.

The Proverbs point up the difference *between hard work and laziness:* "Poor is he who works with a negligent hand, but the hand of the diligent makes rich" (10:4). *Between righteousness and wickedness:* "The memory of the righteous is blessed, but the name of the wicked will rot" (10:7). *Between honesty and dishonesty:* "Truthful lips will be established forever, but a lying tongue is only for a moment" (12:19). *Between humility and arrogance:* "Pride goes before destruction, and a haughty spirit before stumbling. It is better to be humble in spirit with the lowly than to divide the spoil with the proud" (16:18–19).

In fact, discovering what's "better" is a key takeaway of Proverbs, as with everything else the Bible teaches. "Patience is better than power, and controlling one's temper, than capturing a city" (16:32 HCSB). "Better is a little with the fear of the LORD than great treasure and turmoil with it" (15:16). "Better is a dish of vegetables where love is than a fattened ox served with hatred" (15:17). "Better to be a poor man than a liar" (19:22).

In other words, "whatever else you get"—get wisdom.

And from God is where we get that wisdom. He "has made His counsel wonderful and His wisdom great" (Isa. 28:29). "Call to Me," He says, "and I will answer you, and I will tell you great and mighty things, which you do not know" (Jer. 33:3). We can expect to attain on-the-spot wisdom from Him as we ask for it, apply it, and place a high priority on it. Praying for wisdom should become a daily habit and is also a source for developing our prayer strategies.

Wisdom, despite its silver-haired persona, is not an automatic development that kicks in at a certain age. Those who truly desire it can begin living with wisdom at any age—as children, as teenagers, as young adults, as newlyweds, and as new parents. Meanwhile, older men and women who've chosen instead to live a self-seeking, unexamined life, heavy on quick fixes and light on long-term thinking, can end up being more foolish than people half their age.

But God has put His name on the line if wisdom is something you really want. "For the LORD gives wisdom; from His mouth come knowledge and understanding" (Prov. 2:6). "The one who understands a matter finds success, and the one who trusts in the LORD will be happy" (Prov. 16:20 HCSB). "When you lie down, you will not be afraid; you will lie down, and your sleep will be pleasant . . . for the LORD will be your confidence and will keep your foot from a snare" (Prov. 3:24, 26 HCSB).

Pray for it often and expect it promptly. Ask for wisdom. Let it guide your praying, and enjoy its rewards.

Lord, You are my wonderful Counselor and the Source of all wisdom. I take You at Your Word that when I ask for wisdom—from a heart that's ready to put it obediently and faithfully into practice—You will surely pour it out upon me freely. Because I surely need it. Every day in every way. I pray You'd help me view life from Your eternal perspective rather than the world's. Help me think long-term and understand the causes and effects of my choices. Give me the discernment between what is good, better, and best, and help me make right decisions in light of it. In Jesus' name I pray, amen.

25

THE WAYS OF GOD'S SPIRIT

The Spirit searches all things, even the depths of God.
(1 Cor. 2:10)

 Prayer is an admission that we are not in control, and yet at the same time completely and confidently under *God's* control (Ps. 103:19). God knows we often can forget to pray, and not know what to pray or how we should be praying (Rom. 8:26). We can ask for what we know, but still not address the heart of an issue or cover even half of what should be requested. And yet God urges us to keep entering into prayer anyway . . . knowing He can lead us through the One He has deposited into our hearts.

The Holy Spirit is the engine of the Christian life, guiding and empowering us to do what we cannot do on our own. He is the holy, rushing wind of God (John 3:8), breathing life through every part of our prayer lives.

Thanks to His indwelling presence and loving encouragement, our utter helplessness is stabilized by His faithful empowerment and utter provision. Our finite knowledge is surrounded by His infinite wisdom. We offer Him our best work of prayer but trust His Spirit to launch it into far greater works (John 14:12–17).

As you've seen in the last few chapters, God has given His people rich resources to help us strategically pray with power and precision. Having been granted access to His Word, His will, His wisdom, and the wonder of His names, we have an arsenal of weapons to hone our praying to a razor's edge and launch it with pinpoint accuracy.

But still we are inadequate without God's Spirit guiding us. He can guide us to pray for one verse rather than another. To call upon God as *Jehovah Jireh* for provision rather than merely God. To aim at the heart rather than the head of a person in authority. To deal with a sin we've forgotten to confess.

Paul said, "With all prayer and petition pray at all times in the Spirit, and with this in view, be on the alert with all perseverance and petition for all the saints" (Eph. 6:18). This is powerful praying. In the Spirit. At all times. For all the saints.

Every believer in Jesus Christ has the Holy Spirit within them (Eph. 1:13–14). But we must be filled with, submit to, and walk in the Spirit, as opposed to following our sinful flesh. The command to "be filled with the Spirit" (Eph. 5:18) is not just for Christians in charismatic leaning congregations. It is an imperative for every follower of Jesus Christ to obey. The Greek tense used in Ephesians 5:18 is a command to *keep* being filled by God's Spirit. It's not a one-time experience but a moment by moment, daily way of living and submitting and walking in the Spirit (Gal. 5:16–25).

Every morning we should be asking God to fill us with His Spirit as we worship Him and surrender all that we are and have to His loving lordship for the day. Anytime we sin, become bitter, or get in the flesh, we should quickly repent, humble ourselves, and resubmit ourselves to the Lord and to the leading of His Spirit.

When we are abiding in Christ, staying clean and close, and walking in surrendered obedience to Him, we will be much more in tune to the voice of God's Spirit within us. He will be giving us the mind of Christ (1 Cor. 2:16), convicting of sin (John 16:8), producing the fruit of the Spirit in our hearts (Gal. 5:22), leading our decisions (Gal. 5:16–18), and empowering us to be witnesses (Acts 1:8).

"Don't get drunk with wine," Paul said, "which leads to reckless actions." But be similarly "filled by the Spirit" so that you're controlled by Him instead. Overflowing with His joy and hope. Enjoying His peace and contentment. "Singing and making music from your heart to the Lord, giving thanks always for everything . . . in the name of our Lord Jesus Christ" (Eph. 5:18–20 HCSB).

By understanding the Holy Spirit and how He operates, we take our prayers into the ever-flowing stream of God's activity.

He reveals God and His Word to us. Jesus, describing how the Holy Spirit would remain with His disciples after He'd left the earth, identified Him as the "Spirit of truth" (John 14:17)—the "Helper" who "proceeds from the Father" and testifies about the nature of Christ (15:26)—the Guide who "will not speak on His own initiative, but whatever He hears, He will speak; and He will disclose to you what is to come"

(16:13). Even those things which "eye has not seen and ear has not heard," the Spirit is able to reveal to us—what we need to know, *when* we need to know it—"not in words taught by human wisdom, but in those taught by the Spirit, combining spiritual thoughts with spiritual words" (1 Cor. 2:9–13). Through the avenue of humble, believing prayer, He illumines God's Word and makes God's true nature come alive to us, convincing us of spiritual realities—the hideousness of sin, the glories of righteousness, the realities of judgment (John 16:8–11). Reminding us who we are in Christ (Eph. 1:15–19). Comforting us in His love and care.

He prays for us. The "Spirit Himself intercedes for us with groanings too deep for words" (Rom. 8:26). What we *can't pray*, His Spirit can. And therefore we are never without hope or help. It is refreshing to know that God the Father, God the Son, and God the Spirit are three in One. They each know the heart of the other and are in constant communication. While Jesus stands at the right hand of the Father and intercedes for us (Heb. 7:24–25), the Holy Spirit within us is also interceding to the Father on our behalf. "He who searches the hearts knows what the mind of the Spirit is, because He intercedes for the saints according to the will of God" (Rom. 8:27). No one can pray for us better than Jesus and the Holy Spirit. What a blessed privilege to have such perfect prayer partners lovingly interceding for us.

He guides our praying. The Holy Spirit inwardly reminds and leads believers to cry out to our Father in prayer. "For you have not received a spirit of slavery leading to fear again, but you have received a spirit of adoption as sons by which we cry out, 'Abba! Father!'" (Rom. 8:15). You hear people say sometimes how He "speaks" to them. But this speaking is not so much an audible hearing but an internal knowing—a good and timely thought accompanied by a holy burden and a desire to do something specific for the glory of God. It's the Spirit saying to you, "This is the way, walk in it" (Isa. 30:21).

Some people question whether He communicates so personally to us, but the testimony of Scripture seems to indicate otherwise. He alerted Ananias to pray for Saul (Acts 9:10–19), Philip to share with the Ethiopian official (Acts 8:29–30), and us if we will learn to obey Him (Rom. 8:14–16). Sometimes He may bring a person to mind from seemingly out of nowhere, encouraging you to pray for them or reach out to them in love according to their need and His will. Stay open to this kind of prompting, but be aware that the Spirit will never act in contradiction to the Word of God but will always lead you to obey and live out the Word in your personal, real-world circumstances.

Because of the boundless reach, wisdom, and power of the Holy Spirit, He is able to create kingdom connections between you and others in what seem to be the most normal, coincidental happenings of life. So never think of yourself as being hemmed in at the spiritual shoreline, ankle-deep in figuring out His will and His ways on your own. Our prayers are not bound by our limitations because the Spirit has no limits, and He is living within us.

Lord, thank You for sending Your Spirit to lead me and guide me and fill me with Your wisdom and insight. Just as You've sent Him here to testify to Christ through Your people on the earth, I pray that my heart will desire Him for that very reason—that my life will bear living witness to Jesus. Fill me with Your Spirit. Teach me to walk in Your Spirit and pray in the Spirit. Everywhere I go. With everyone I encounter. In every place be glorified in me.

26

PRAYING OFFENSIVELY

They go from strength to strength.
(Ps. 84:7)

 Part of a good prayer strategy is knowing how to pray against evil. We all know, of course, the dangers that lurk within temptation. We're well familiar with the enemy's arrows of fear, anger, lust, and jealousy. But in this section we will focus on going on the offense in a positive way, meaning praying for the advancement of light, love, and truth.

Near the beginning of the model prayer, Jesus taught us to pray for three very important things: "Thy kingdom come. Thy will be done in earth, as it is in heaven. Give us this day our daily bread" (Matt. 6:10–11 KJV). All good things to pray *for*, not just things to pray *against*. So the Christian life is not merely about staying away from sin. It's also about walking in love with God and others. We're not only praying against the gates of hell but praying for heaven on earth. We want God's kingdom to expand and His will to be done. And only part of this task involves stopping the enemy and standing firm in the evil day.

Sure, there are times when we need to play defense. But not *all* the time. We need a game plan for offense as well—asking God to open doors for the gospel, to send forth laborers into the harvest field, to pour out His Holy Spirit in revival, to fill us with His love and the knowledge of His will, to use our spiritual gifts in His service, and to raise up a generation who will honor His name. Spiritual warfare is about standing our ground against the enemy *and* taking new ground for the kingdom.

Matthew 5:16 states, "Let your light shine before men in such a way that they may see your good works, and glorify your Father who is in heaven." Think of your marriage, family, or city, and consider your answers these questions generate . . .

What is the most loving thing I can ask for right now?

What could I pray for that would be overwhelmingly good?

What could greatly advance God's kingdom in my situation?

What could I pray for that would be really glorifying to God?

We find positive prayers and steps for taking ground all through Scripture. In fact, God wants to help us and give us gifts along the way to encourage and assist us. Jesus tells us in Matthew 7:11, "If you then, being evil, know how to give good gifts to your children, how much more will your Father who is in heaven give what is good to those who ask Him!"

When we love someone, we want nothing but the best for them. John prays this type of prayer in 3 John 2, saying,

"Beloved, I pray that in all respects you may prosper and be in good health, just as your soul prospers."

If God is good and is preparing good things for us, then we need to be actively seeking and asking for these things. Praying very loving prayers. We need to cover situations in prayer and ask God to bless, provide, and be glorified as much as possible . . . praying that He would do more than we can ask or imagine. Why? Because His glory is the ultimate goal of all praying.

Not to mention that one of the best defenses is a great offense.

So don't just pray against hardship, but pray for blessings also. Instead of merely praying against a divorce, for instance, ask God to make your marriage a beautiful picture of the gospel of Christ and His love for His bride, and that He will use you to minister to others and advance the kingdom through your loving relationship as husband and wife. Instead of praying that your church leaders won't fight during a business meeting, pray for loving unity and revival to break out, resulting in greater ministry opportunities.

Scripture says in Romans 12:21, "Do not be overcome by evil, but overcome evil with good." The apostle Paul was a great example of this mind-set when praying for his new brothers and sisters in the faith. He wrote in long, uplifting terms in Colossians 1:9–12, "We have not ceased to pray for you and to ask that you may be filled with the knowledge of His will in all spiritual wisdom and understanding, so that you will walk in a manner worthy of the Lord, to please Him in all respects, bearing fruit in every good work and increasing in the knowledge of God; strengthened with all power, according to His glorious might, for the attaining of all steadfastness and patience; joyously giving thanks to the Father, who has qualified us to share in the inheritance of the saints in Light."

Wouldn't you want something prayed over you like that? To be filled with knowledge, wisdom, and an understanding of God's will? To bear much fruit in your life for God's glory?

This is how to pray proactively and go on the offense. Paul gives us more examples in Philippians 1:9–11, saying, "And this I pray, that your love may abound still more and more in real knowledge and all discernment, so that you may approve the things that are excellent, in order to be sincere and blameless until the day of Christ; having been filled with the fruit of righteousness which comes through Jesus Christ, to the glory and praise of God."

Jesus also prayed lovingly for Himself, His disciples, and future believers in John 17 by praying that God would be glorified through Him and them. Praying that God would save and protect those who believe in Him as the Christ. Praying that they would be filled with joy and come together in unity. Praying that the world would know that God sent Him to save the lost.

So the next time you face a tough situation, or are just spending daily time with the Lord in prayer, remember to pray both defensively and offensively. Stand on the Word of God when under attack, but also ask God specifically for good things to happen in your life and in the lives of those you're praying for. Above all, pray that God would get the glory. So as you plan your prayer times, feel free to ask God to do something really, really good!

> *Lord, thank You for giving me prayer to help push back against the darkness. But thank You, too, for enabling me to use prayer as a way of inviting Your blessing, enjoying Your presence, and actively investing lovingly in others' lives. For while Your strength and power amaze me, Lord, Your love amazes me even more . . . because I know what I'm like; I know what I deserve. Yet You continually take care of me and transform me. You keep turning my negatives into positives. You keep giving me opportunities to win. To advance. To conquer. And for this, I praise Your name.*

27

PRAYING PREEMPTIVELY

*Keep watching and praying that you may not
enter into temptation. (Matt. 26:41)*

 If you were the leader of a country and discovered you would soon be attacked by a brutal, invading army, what would you do? If no terms of peace were possible, you would do everything plausible to quickly prepare for war. Evaluating resources. Developing strategies. Stationing troops.

This is also what we must do in prayer. We must first fight our battles on our knees before the battle rages in the natural realm. The Bible says we have a real spiritual enemy who is out to steal, kill, and destroy us.

Jesus Himself recognized Satan, the devil. Christ repeatedly resisted and rebuked him throughout His ministry. The Bible says, "The Son of God appeared for this purpose, to destroy the works of the devil" (1 John 3:8).

As some have mistakenly claimed, Satan is not merely a catch-all symbol of evil. Not a mere fable. More than a dozen books of the Bible specifically reference Satan by name. Jesus said, "I watched Satan fall from heaven like a lightning flash" (Luke 10:18 HCSB). The apostles and first churches were repeatedly forced to stand against him. And until Christ returns and is reigning on the earth, we must stay on alert and overcome him by the blood of the lamb and the word of our testimony (Rev. 12:11; 20:1–10).

He is real. He is evil. He is crafty.

Peter learned this the hard way. Early on, Jesus taught him to preemptively pray, "Do not bring us into temptation, but deliver us from the evil one" (Matt 6:13 HCSB). Then on the night of Christ's betrayal, Jesus warned him, "Behold, Satan has demanded permission to sift you like wheat; but I have prayed for you" (Luke 22:31–32). Later that same evening, Jesus instructed him to "keep watching and praying that you may not enter into temptation; the spirit is willing, but the flesh is weak" (Matt. 26:41). But Peter fell asleep instead. A few minutes later, he was awakened off guard. Peter emotionally overreacted, hacked off a man's ear, abandoned Jesus, and then adamantly denied Christ three times instead of being loyal like he had passionately promised a few hours earlier. He never prayed preemptively, and so he wept bitterly. He was devastated and depressed for days until Christ restored him.

"A prudent man foresees evil and hides himself, but the simple pass on and are punished" (Prov. 22:3 NKJV).

We must learn to pray preemptively, lifting our calendars, commitments, and coming opportunities to the Lord. Spiritually fastening our armor and asking God to guide, provide, empower, and protect us before stepping into the heat of combat.

One thing that will help you is to understand how the enemy attacks. His playbook and patterns have been the same for millennia. If you already know his moves, you can prepare and pray more specifically beforehand. His signature schemes include the following:

Distraction. Misdirection is Warfare 101. David wrote, "I am restless in my complaint and am surely distracted, because of the voice of the enemy" (Ps. 55:2–3). Satan will constantly try to get you off track. To focus on even good things which are not God's best things. Many times in Scripture we see good and kind people lured away from God's purposes to waste time on side issues. While Jesus was serving the last Passover meal and began alerting His disciples to His coming death, they were in a sidebar dispute about which of them was the greatest (Luke 22:24). While He was sharing His heart at Martha's house, she couldn't stop rattling the pots and pans in the kitchen to pause and hear His vital messages (Luke 10:41–42). In our day of digital demands, the enemy can easily distract us by suggesting in our heads that we chase the ding of a text, the latest buzz, or another two-minute viral video. A hundred times a day. Even while praying, he would love to get us focused on our To-Do list and the worries of the day instead of the Lord. So our Lord repeatedly warns us, "Watch and pray. Stay on the alert."

Deception. Jesus said whenever Satan speaks a lie (which is all the time), "he speaks from his own nature, for he is a liar and the father of lies" (John 8:44). Strongholds, addictions, and sins are founded upon lies. They are a perversion of God's truth. Promises never delivered. False advertising.

Sin will fail you, let you down, and leave you empty. But his temptations brazenly try to assure you that if you act now, your situation will be different. It won't affect you like it does other people. He displays the pleasure and hides the consequences. That's why you can't ever believe him. But too often we do . . . if we don't keep ourselves "serious and disciplined for prayer" (1 Pet. 4:7 HCSB). We are not strong enough to stand against his deceptions unless we're on our knees, staying instructed in what is actually true. He will lie to you about God's goodness, the Bible's trustworthiness, who you really are, and what is morally right and wrong. He'll use lies to puff you up in pride or condemn you into the depths of depression. Which brings us to . . .

Derision. When he's not lying, he's usually running you down or running down someone else in your mind. Bringing up things from your past. Falsely presuming someone else's guilt. Yes, you've been forgiven in the blood of Christ, yet he keeps you scraping old wounds. Inciting doubt. He's the "accuser of our brethren" (Rev. 12:10), accusing you of not being good enough, even though that's why Christ came in love to save you. In order for you to deflect these accusations, you need to be studying the Word, finding your identity in Christ, and praying for wisdom and discernment. That's how you throw out his trumped-up charges.

Division. One hallmark of the gospel is the loving unity it brings to people of all nations, all backgrounds, all ages, and demographics. All in Christ. One in Christ. But Satan knows "if a house is divided against itself, that house will not be able to stand" (Mark 3:25). Anger and argument among God's people may not *destroy* the gospel, but they can destroy your testimony and effectiveness in sharing it. Disunity paints Christians and our faith as being weak, hypocritical, and phony. When husbands and wives are at odds, when children and their parents clash, when the pastor and his deacon-possessed church quarrel, you can be sure the main culprit is actually the one you can't see. Stirring up division. Sowing discord among brethren. Encouraging us to presume the worst instead of praying for the best.

We must not live foolishly "ignorant of his devices" (2 Cor. 2:11 NKJV). We should pray for God to help us stay focused on His will, for His Holy Spirit to keep us walking in truth, for false accusations to be thrown down, and for love and unity to reign in our relationships.

This is what the spiritual armor of Ephesians 6 is for. "Truth" to wrap around our waist, dispelling his lies. "Righteousness"—from Christ—worn across our chests and lived out in bold, active, grateful obedience. "Peace" in our daily walk, not rattled by Satan's accusations and distractions. "Faith" as a shield to fend off his attacks. "Salvation" guarding our minds from being convinced we've failed God too badly to be saved. "The word of God," wielded like a sword, slicing through the enemy's distortions. And to activate them, we "pray"—staying "on the alert with all perseverance and petition for all the saints" (Eph. 6:14–18). We're all in this together. And prayer is how we do it. It's what unites us. It helps protect us.

Nehemiah's rebuilding of the walls of Jerusalem was characterized by numerous, ankle-biting annoyances that never let up. He reported how his detractors "mocked us and despised us" (Neh. 2:19), becoming "furious and very angry" (4:1), conspiring together to "come and fight against Jerusalem and to cause a disturbance in it" (4:8). So Nehemiah and his fellow workmen were forced to work with one hand while holding a weapon in the other. They spent their nights laboring in shifts and standing guard for one another against the threats. But because he consistently prayed, Nehemiah consistently discerned and avoided being distracted and deceived by their schemes.

Don't think for a second that our day or task is any different. "Be of sober spirit," Peter said, "be on the alert. Your adversary, the devil, prowls around like a roaring lion, seeking someone to devour. But resist him, firm in your faith" (1 Pet. 5:8–9).

Nonetheless, the question is not whether he's coming out to engage you in battle. Seen or unseen. The question is whether you're going to prepare in prayer first or wait until the devil has you in a headlock before you call on the One who has already defeated him.

By preemptively preparing, we will ensure that we do a lot more winning than losing. We'll know what's happening and beat him to the punch. And we'll "watch and pray" on the alert and be victorious by God's strength.

Lord, thank You for alerting us in Your Word to the tactics and activity of the devil. Thank You also for equipping us with spiritual weaponry to stand firm and push back against his assaults and his campaign of lies, distortions, distractions, and accusations. Help us not be ignorant of his schemes. Give us the grace to discern

THE BATTLE PLAN FOR PRAYER

how the enemy will try to attack so we can wisely pray preemptively and prepare ourselves to stand firm in the evil day. Keep us steady, Lord, clear-minded, braced, ready, walking wisely and living in victory. Fix our eyes upon You by faith, kept by Your power. In Jesus' name, amen.

28

PRAYING DEFENSIVELY

Be strong in the Lord and in the strength of His might. Put
on the full armor of God, so that you will be able to stand
firm against the schemes of the devil. (Eph. 6:10–11)

 When the Japanese attacked Pearl Harbor in December 1941, the American base was equipped with multiple battleships, cruisers, destroyers, and anti-aircraft guns. Yet 2,400 Americans were killed, nearly 1,300 wounded, and much of their naval fleet wiped out. The defensive firepower had been on hand. Yet those under attack weren't ready to use them.

In like manner, Christians are equipped with everything needed for life and godliness (2 Pet. 1:3), but many are not ready when the enemy attacks. So they continually live in defeat in one or more areas of their lives. The last chapter was about preemptively praying before shots are fired. Today's strategy, however, is a hand-to-hand battle plan to use immediately when Satan strikes.

God's Word says spiritual war is taking place around you. So you must take up "the shield of faith with which you will be able to extinguish all the flaming arrows of the evil

172

one. And take the helmet of salvation, and the sword of the Spirit, which is the word of God. With all prayer and petition pray at all times in the Spirit" (Eph. 6:16–18).

The following R.E.S.P.O.N.D. acronym is a powerful, biblically based battle plan to help you strategically respond to a personal attack of the enemy. This can be used anytime the devil starts tempting you to lust, fear, or live in condemnation. It also works when discouragement climbs on your shoulders, sin is being rationalized, or lies are trying to take root in your heart. When the devil attacks, the first thing you should do is . . .

1. *RESIST Satan in Jesus' name.* "Resist the devil and he will flee from you" (James 4:7). We don't have to put up with Satan's taunts, accusations, or mind games. Jesus refused to be bribed into surrendering control or falling victim to his schemes. Christ pushed back. He said, "Go away, Satan!" on one occasion (Matt. 4:10 HCSB) and "Get behind Me, Satan!" on another (Mark 8:33). We should do the same thing, but we do so in Christ's name and by His authority, not our own.

The name of Jesus Christ is above every other name (Phil. 2:9–10). His is the name in which we pray, are healed (Acts 3:6), and cast out demons (Matt. 7:22; Mark 9:38–39). There's a reason why the name "Jesus Christ" is used for cursing and profanity in movies and television, and never Buddha or Muhammad . . . because it is the name of power that Satan must submit to and wants to dishonor. We should never speak Jesus' name irreverently. It is holy. His name saves us and keeps us out of hell (Acts 4:12; Rom. 10:9–10). God's identity, character, and reputation stand behind it. So when you are confronted in combat with the devil, resist him by calling on the most powerful name known to man. Either confront him directly with, "Go away Satan, in Jesus' name" or indirectly in prayer, "Father, in Jesus' name, I ask You to rebuke Satan" (Jude 9). He must flee!

2. *ESCAPE with Scripture.* God promises to always provide a "way of escape" from temptation (1 Cor. 10:13). Every time Jesus was tempted by the devil (Luke 4:1–13), He raised His shield of faith and strategically cut down Satan with the sword of the Spirit by quoting the Word of God (Eph. 6:17). We should trust and utilize an appropriate verse that deals with the specific temptation or deception at hand (Matt. 4:1–11). God has given us a fully loaded cache of powerful ammunition in Scripture, ready to fire at the enemy. You just need to learn verses that deal with your issues so when Satan tempts or plants a wicked thought in your head, like "You are unloved and will fail!" you can respond with, "Get away from me, Satan, in Jesus' name. Romans 5:8 says God proved His love for me when Christ died for me. And Philippians 4:13 says "I can do all things through Christ who strengthens me!" (NKJV). Block, counter punch, and kick to the face! (See page 242 for a list of spiritual ammo you can utilize.)

3. *SEARCH for unconfessed sin.* Times of testing should become catalysts for cleansing. The book of James says, after you've submitted to God and resisted the devil, you should "cleanse your hands, sinners, and purify your hearts" (James 4:8 HCSB). Victory necessitates repentance. Repentance helps you stand strong against temptation.

But there's a difference between being *tempted* by something and being tormented by something. Everyone is tempted. Jesus was. You will be. It's not a sin to be tempted. But if the enemy is constantly tormenting you with something, there's a good chance unconfessed sin from your past has given him a foothold of operation he's using to establish a stronghold (a network of lies) in your heart (2 Cor. 10:3–5). Though the truth will set us free, lies can keep us in bondage. We must throw off any hindrance of sin "which so easily entangles us" (Heb. 12:1) and the lies that go with it so we can walk in the victory and freedom Christ has already won for us on the cross.

The enemy's attacks today may or may not be because of yesterday's sin. Regardless, we should pray, "Search me, O God, and know my heart; test me and know my anxious thoughts. See if there is any offensive way in me, and lead me in the way everlasting" (Ps. 139:23–24 NIV). Then if God reveals an area of unrepentant sin from yesterday or even a decade ago, quickly admit it and empty yourself of it. Go back to where the ground was first given and confess what gave it up.

4. *PLEAD the blood of Jesus.* When we admit sin and plead (appeal by faith) for God to cleanse us by His blood, He is faithful to forgive and wash us from all unrighteousness (1 John 1:7–9). But we should rest in this. Forgiven believers who don't believe they are forgiven will not act like believers. Easy marks for enemy fire. It's true, "All have sinned and fall short of the glory of God"—no doubt. But by faith in Him, we've been "justified as a gift by His grace through the redemption which is in Christ Jesus . . . in His

blood" (Rom. 3:23–25). Only His blood washes away sin. If God says you are forgiven, do not call Him a liar in your heart by believing you are not. The Lord told Peter, "Do not call anything impure that God has made clean" (Acts 10:15 NIV).

The devil might continue steady accusations against this truth as part of his overall attack. But just because he says something and you believe it doesn't make it any more accurate. Cling to the unalterable settings of Scripture when your emotional compass readings are spinning around the dial. There is power in the blood. Plead it. Ask for it. Trust it. Move to the safe fortress of faith where your cleansing has already been assured. Pray, "Father, I plead for You to cover me and cleanse me with the blood of Jesus. I trust Your faithfulness and rest in Your forgiveness."

5. *OVERTAKE ground given to Satan.* In spiritual warfare, we are wrestling against "principalities and powers" (Col. 2:15 KJV)—rulers of darkness who claim jurisdiction. But through the cross, Jesus fully disarmed the power of the enemy (Col. 2:8–15). So Satan no longer has bullets in his gun. But he still bluffs and deceives people into submitting to him.

When you sin or believe his lie, you are yielding control and giving him ground (John 8:34; Eph. 4:26–27). But as you repent and believe the truth, he loses control over you (2 Tim. 2:24–26). As you cast down his lies and any wicked imaginations from your own heart, you also need to ask God to be Lord over you and occupy those former areas with His Spirit and His Word. That's how you bring every thought "captive to the obedience of Christ" (2 Cor. 10:5).

So at this point, present yourself back to God and rededicate yourself completely to the lordship of Christ. Ask Him to take back full control of every part of you so you can love Him with *all* of your heart, mind, soul, and strength. And pray that He would strengthen and enable you to keep advancing across ground He's already died to claim.

6. *NAME someone in targeted prayer.* After the apostle Paul discussed the sword of the Spirit, he said we should get busy praying for others (Eph. 6:17–19).

But not only does this strategy help others; it helps us as well. Instead of continuing to wrestle with a temptation or a lie or on "not sinning," we can just refocus on interceding for others.

If you're being tempted by a lustful thought, for example, then resist the devil, escape with the Word, deal with past sins, rededicate your mind to God, and *then* start praying for and thanking God for your spouse (or future spouse). When tempted by discouragement, pray for your pastor or someone dealing with depression. Greed? Pray for your children to be grateful. Prayer allows you to climb off the endless worry-go-round and experience the "peace of God" that can "guard your hearts and your minds in Christ Jesus" (Phil. 4:6–7).

7. *DELIGHT in the Lord.* "And now my head will be lifted up above my enemies around me, and I will offer in His tent sacrifices with shouts of joy; I will sing, yes, I will sing praises to the LORD" (Ps. 27:6). Now it's time to celebrate what just happened. The enemy approached. He brought his worst. He bore down with all his weight. But in Christ, you stood firm. You resisted, counterattacked, and

defeated him without stumbling. Even on ground where you've so often fallen before and been taken prisoner, you whipped him and lived to tell about it. You responded with the Word. You made it. *God did it.* Praise the Lord!

And doesn't that feel amazingly better than before? Remember, "a righteous man falls seven times, and rises again" (Prov. 24:16). Be thankful for that. But who says you can't march ahead with one victory after another, gaining momentum, actually experiencing the free, abundant life you've been promised? You can.

1. **R** ESIST Satan in Jesus' name
2. **E** SCAPE with Scripture
3. **S** EARCH for unconfessed sin
4. **P** LEAD the blood of Jesus
5. **O** VERTAKE ground given to Satan
6. **N** AME someone in targeted prayer
7. **D** ELIGHT in the Lord

If you will learn this and do this, the devil will tempt you less and less when he realizes his attacks only remind you more to call on Jesus, quote Scripture, repent, pray, and praise.

Learn how to R.E.S.P.O.N.D. And let *Satan* be the one who's in for a surprise.

Lord, I thank You that You are greater in me than he who is in the world. Thank You for paving the way and not leaving me here to fight my battles alone. Thank You for showing Yourself more than capable of giving me everything needed. Help me walk in the victory You have already won on the cross. Please give me the wisdom and grace to overcome every lie, stronghold, addiction, and area of defeat in my life. Teach me how to be strong in the Lord and in His mighty power. Help me put on the full armor of God and to stand firm in the evil day. I am confident in You and in how much I need You. In Jesus' name I pray, amen.

29

PRAYING
EXTRAORDINARILY

*I sought the Lord in my day of trouble. My hands were
continually lifted up all night long. (Ps. 77:2 HCSB)*

 Prayer strategies go to the next level when
situations reach a point of desperation. Like
when a mother is rushed to the hospital with
a premature delivery. Like when the foreclo-
sure notice is said to be on its way over. When
the fighting is so bad, you're finally starting to
seriously believe your family will not stay intact.

These unexpected moments of intensity call for radical,
drop-everything prayer. Phone-your-friends praying. Rally
the church. *Everybody* praying. But just because you're desperate doesn't mean you shouldn't be strategic. Sometimes
even more so.

The experience of Esther in the Old Testament led to the
necessity for extraordinary prayer. You may recall how she, a
beautiful young Jewish woman, was selected as a candidate
for queen of Persia when King Ahasuerus deposed his own
wife. But from inside the palace, Esther learned from her

childhood guardian, Mordecai, about a plan to exterminate the Jewish people. All of them.

The situation was dire—no less for Esther than anyone else. She wasn't yet in a position to approach the king with any petition without permission. Customs of the day meant she could be lawfully killed for attempting to enter his presence. But she made a courageous call for extraordinary prayer: "Go, assemble all the Jews who are found in Susa, and fast for me; do not eat or drink for three days, night or day. I and my maidens also will fast in the same way. And thus I will go in to the king, which is not according to law; and if I perish, I perish" (Esth. 4:16).

The result of their united, above-and-beyond praying was miraculous. The mastermind of the genocide was killed instead, hanged on his own gallows. And Mordecai, the Jew, was raised to a key position of leadership, charged with the state-sanctioned program of *protecting* the Jews from further persecution.

That's the kind of prayer model the Bible guides us to follow.

Notice they prayed *corporately*. Extraordinary prayer is a team effort. Following Jesus' ascension to heaven, the eleven remaining apostles in Acts 1 sped back to Jerusalem and gathered in an upper room to pray. There "with one mind" they were "continually devoting themselves to prayer" (v. 14). When Peter was later thrown into prison under heavy guard, "prayer for him was being made fervently by the church to God" (Acts 12:5). The night before his execution, chained between two soldiers, Peter was trying to sleep. Then an angel appeared, set him free, and led him past the guards and gates on his way back home. As one old-time author has said, "The angel fetched Peter out of prison, but it was prayer that fetched the angel."

They prayed with *fasting*. We've mentioned fasting earlier, listing it as one of the "keys" of prayer. But serious matters call for unusual sacrifice with focused devotion and dedication. God, through the prophet Joel, commanded His people to return to Him "with all your heart . . . with fasting, weeping and mourning" (Joel 2:12). Jesus, at the outset of His earthly ministry, prepared Himself for the challenges ahead by committing to forty days of fasting (Matt. 4:2). We don't say no to ourselves or our appetites easily. But by denying the daily demands of our flesh in order to focus all of our attention on God, we can go more deeply and intently into focused prayer in times of difficulty, strain, and emergency. We fast because we mean business. Fasting together means we're united in appealing to Him and hearing from Him. And when it's done in sincerity, God consistently honors it.

They prayed *fervently*. Persistently and passionately. Circumstances can reach a point where the survival instinct alone can produce fervent praying. When the men on board ship with the prophet Jonah began fearing for their lives, they called "earnestly" on a God they didn't even know, begging for mercy from the storm (Jonah 1:14). God spared them. When the recipients of Jonah's message in Nineveh fell under frightening conviction because of their sins, they too called "earnestly" on God that He would spare them from destruction (Jonah 3:8). God spared them.

But many conditions in our world and personal lives today are just as worthy of alarm, calling equally as much for fervent prayer. Sins in our nation. Pride in our churches. Heartbreak in our homes. Persecution among our brothers and sisters. Need and want of drastic proportions that we don't want to see and don't want to think about. The seeds of hardship and hostility against Christians—experienced even now in many nations of the world—are already here on our shores. But is the church of God broken and surrendered? Are we willing to "be miserable and mourn and weep" when necessary? (James 4:9). To let our hearts beat with His? Prepared to be loyal to Him in all situations? Devoted to Him and Him alone—enough for us to be praying as one body, united in long seasons of agonizing desire for God's favor and His mercy?

We know without a doubt that "in the last days difficult times will come" (2 Tim. 3:1). Jesus realistically told His disciples, "You will have suffering in this world" (John 16:33 HCSB). "Do not be surprised," Peter said, "at the fiery ordeal among you" (1 Pet. 4:12). They are sometimes indicative of satanic plots, and sometimes just the result of sin's cancer on the world, making us hungry for the perfected glory of life forever with the Lord. But when these problems reach an insurmountable breaking point, they require unusual power that will only result from extraordinary prayer.

All of us tend to revert to a default level of praying—most likely an easier and more comfortable praying than we'd like to admit. But Jesus, in His own life, would ramp up the fervency of His praying depending on the need of the moment. From a joyful request, to praying all night, to crying out "Abba! Father!" on His face before going to the cross (Mark 14:36).

Fervent prayer touches God's heart. And "the effective, fervent prayer of a righteous man avails much" (James 5:16 NKJV). But imagine what the combined, persistent, united prayers of many righteous people, each of them fasting and praying, might accomplish. It doesn't just connect. It works miracles, moves mountains, ushers in revival, and changes the course of nations. Extraordinary prayer can yield extraordinary results.

Lord God Almighty, I praise You that nothing is impossible with You. Train us and lead us into extraordinary prayer. Help us throw off any sin, surrendering ourselves completely to You. May we see the needs of our city and nation the way You see them. Unite believers in my church and community in extraordinary prayer. May we walk in love, agree in heart, fast in faith, and unite in fervent, persistent prayer. Bring revival and spiritual awakening to our land. Be glorified through us, O God!

NEHEMIAH'S PRAYER

The situation at the beginning of the book of Nehemiah called for extraordinary prayer. It came with several of the same characteristics as some of the high-pressure situations you've faced in your own life (and perhaps are facing even now): a need for quick action, an upset family member, a seemingly helpless desire to do something, lack of proximity to the actual location of the problem, dependence on someone else's favor or decision before being able to take the next step, and more.

But even with the frustrating presence of all these moving parts—and the readily available option of either giving up or getting angry—he chose instead the best solution: *prayer.*

When we take a closer look at what he said and did in bringing his distress to God, we see the strategy of extraordinary prayer in expert action. In the space of just five or six verses, he did about two dozen things exactly right when he prayed. Let's look at them closely for a minute. Read his prayer from Nehemiah 1:4–11, and notice the parts we've highlighted in italics. Then refer to the chart on the next page, seeing the specific prayer strategies and principles he was using, all in this one prayer.

"When I heard these words, *I sat down* and *wept and mourned* for days; and *I was fasting and praying* before the God of heaven.

"I said, *'I beseech You, O Lord God of heaven,* the *great and awesome God, who preserves the covenant and lovingkindness* for those who love Him and keep His commandments, let Your ear now be attentive and Your eyes open to hear the prayer of Your servant which *I am praying* before You now, *day and night, on behalf of the sons of Israel* Your servants, confessing the sins of the sons of Israel which *we have sinned* against You; *I and my father's house have sinned*. We have acted very corruptly against You and have not kept the commandments, nor the statutes, nor the ordinances which You commanded Your servant Moses.

"*Remember the word* which You commanded Your servant Moses, saying, 'If you are unfaithful I will scatter you among the peoples; but if you return to Me and keep My commandments and do them, though those of you who have been scattered were in the most remote part of the heavens, I will gather them from there and will bring them to the place where I have chosen to cause *My name to dwell.'* They are Your servants and Your people whom You redeemed by *Your great power and by Your strong hand.*

"*O Lord, I beseech You,* may Your ear be attentive to the *prayer of Your servant* and the *prayer of Your servants* who delight to *revere Your name,* and *make Your servant successful today* and *grant him compassion* before this man."

Nehemiah's Words	How He Prayed
"I sat down"	with humility
"wept and mourned"	with brokenness
"I was fasting and praying"	with fasting
"I beseech You, O Lord [Yahweh]	using God's name
"God [Elohim] of heaven"	using another of God's names
"great and awesome"	praising God's character
"God" [El]	using another of God's names
"who preserves covenant, lovingkindness"	praising God's attributes
"praying day and night"	with fervency and persistence
"on behalf of the sons of Israel"	with intercession
"we have sinned"	confessing sin, interceding
"I and my father's house have sinned"	with personal repentance
"remember the word"	praying God's Word
"[God's] name to dwell"	using God's name
"Your great power and strong hand"	with praise and faith
"O Lord" [Adonai]	yet another of God's names
"I beseech you"	supplication
"prayer of Your servant"	individual praying
"prayer of Your servants"	united praying
"revere Your name"	using God's name
"make your servant successful"	praying specifically
"grant him compassion"	with faith and expectation

30

PRAYING FOR THE LOST

We plead on Christ's behalf, "Be reconciled to God."
(2 Cor. 5:20 HCSB)

 If we're honest, we probably pray for ourselves more than we pray for anyone else. After all, who among our friends and family knows our hopes, struggles, and concerns more completely than we do? Our next prayer targets, after ourselves, are most likely the people closest to us, followed by other friends and relatives.

But as believers, how much of a priority should we be placing on praying for the lost—those who haven't put faith in Jesus Christ and established a relationship with Him?

In Romans 10, Paul said his heart's desire and prayer was for the salvation of his people. Then in 1 Timothy 2:4, we learn that God wants "all men to be saved and to come to the knowledge of the truth." Even John 3:16, which may be the most recognizable verse from Scripture, proclaims that God's love motivated Him to send His Son for the salvation of people all over the world.

So there's no question God is pleased and glorified when people turn to Him and receive Him by faith through Jesus

Christ. But since that's the case, and since we know God "reconciled us to Himself through Christ and gave us the ministry of reconciliation" (2 Cor. 5:18 HCSB), then why aren't we praying fervently and faithfully to that end?

One reason is because the enemy stands against us and our prayers. His plan is to prevent as many people as possible from hearing and receiving the good news of the gospel. For "if our gospel is veiled, it is veiled to those who are perishing, in whose case the god of this world has blinded the minds of the unbelieving so that they might not see the light of the gospel of the glory of Christ, who is the image of God" (2 Cor. 4:3–4). Satan knows he's lost this war. His desire now is simply to cause as much damage as he can . . . *while* he can.

But we can stand against him in prayer, asking God to open the eyes of the lost and reveal to them their need for a Savior, asking Him to send us and others to tell them about His love and forgiveness. Through our gentle, patient, clear testimony and lifestyle as believers, Paul said, "Perhaps God may grant them repentance leading to the knowledge of the truth, and they may come to their senses and escape from the snare of the devil, having been held captive by him to do his will" (2 Tim. 2:25–26).

In other words, our prayers against the enemy's tactics, along with our obedience to Christ, can create opportunities for more people to hear and understand the truth of the gospel. That's why we hear Paul asking the church of his day, "Devote yourselves to prayer, keeping alert in it with an attitude of thanksgiving; praying at the same time for us as well, that God will open up to us a door for the word, so that we may speak forth the mystery of Christ, for which I have also been imprisoned; that I may make it clear in the way I ought to speak" (Col. 4:2–4).

God can be trusted to grant us these "open doors" to share testimony of how Christ has changed our life, setting the stage for the gospel to penetrate others' hearts as well. He knows best how to grant these moments, of course. Once we pray and are looking for them, we won't have any trouble spotting them. But we must be ready and willing to take advantage of them when they appear.

This leads us to the next part of our prayer strategy: *readiness.*

When the time comes to open our mouths and speak, we need the boldness to say what ought to be said. Paul pled in Ephesians 6:19 (HCSB), "Pray also for me, that the message may be given to me when I open my mouth to make known with boldness the mystery of the gospel." We need the same kind of readiness and confidence. We can't clam up and allow embarrassment or the fear of rejection to stop us from sharing the most important message in the universe. Putting our insecurities above another's need for hearing the truth is like saying, "My comfort level is more important to me than your salvation."

That's why Paul prayed for boldness. It's why we should pray for boldness too—not to overwhelm people by our intensity but so we won't back down from saying what God leads us to say, with the right heart and demeanor. Then the Holy Spirit can do what only He can do: *bring repentance.*

Jesus Himself said the reason He came to earth was to seek and save the lost (Luke 19:10). And as part of His body on the earth today, we need to view this same priority as a crucial part of our purpose as well. Not that we should deny our God-given responsibilities to become full-time evangelists, but in everything we do, in every situation, we need to be ready to share the love of Christ with a lost, dying world.

Our prayers shouldn't be limited, however, only to those within our area of influence. We must also pray for people we'll never meet. Pray for missionaries to be given the boldness and opportunity to share God's love with as many people as possible in lands we may never visit. Pray for leaders to hear the gospel and realize their need for forgiveness and salvation as they guide others. Pray for those in the spotlight who influence the masses. Pray for unreached people groups who desperately need someone to come acquaint them with the hope that's found only in Christ. Yes, pray for everyone, everywhere, on an ongoing basis. God will know how to take even our general, global prayers and invest them in all the right places, directly into the hearts of those He's already drawing toward Himself.

So how do we pray for the lost? We pray for God to begin working in their hearts to prepare them to receive the truth.

We pray against the enemy, that he would be prevented from blinding their eyes and hearts.

We pray for opportunities and boldness, both for ourselves and others, to share the gospel with them in power and love.

We pray for conviction of sin to agitate their hearts, bringing about true repentance and a desire for Christ's cleansing.

And we pray for God's blessing, guidance, protection, and presence to be on all those who obey Him and seek Him.

When we realize the lost are spiritually blind, hopeless, and perishing without Christ—just as all of us were, before He reached out in love to rescue us—this awareness should raise our urgency to pray. Because time is limited. Our opportunities may be limited as well. So let's obey what God has called us to do, seeking the one lost sheep, the one lost coin, the one prodigal who doesn't yet understand the truth (Luke 15). Pray for God to put people in our path, giving us open doors as well as the Christlike courage to speak as we should. Support those who share His love both in our country and overseas, covering them in prayer, eager to see God glorified in bringing the incredible gift of salvation to the lost. "For everyone who calls on the name of the Lord will be saved," as the Word boldly and freely declares (Rom. 10:13 HCSB). And we get to be part of it. Through prayer.

Lord, give me a greater heart for the lost—a heart that doesn't ignore them or work around them, but rather breaks for them. Hurts for them. Guard me from even subtly downplaying their need for You or considering their salvation someone else's job to worry about. Open my eyes as I travel throughout each day, watching for You to open doors so I can give effective testimony to Your goodness and faithfulness. And do battle against our enemy, O Lord, that he would not succeed in blocking the truth from getting through to those who are dying without it, without You. Thank You for allowing me to be part of this kingdom priority. Help me see it as a privilege, not a burden—a willing sacrifice for the incredible sacrifice You've made for me.

31

PRAYING FOR BELIEVERS

*The hearts of the saints have been
refreshed through you. (Philem. 7)*

Perhaps some of the most commonly spoken words from one Christian to another are "I'll be praying for you." And yet perhaps the most commonly *unspoken* words are the prayers that would have been said if those promises were truly kept.

We need each other's prayers. It's one of the most loving things you could ever do for each other. Your brothers and sisters in Christ, at any challenging point in their lives, need to be able to take a deep breath and realize they're not alone, that their Christian family has their back. They need the assurance that you and others are praying. Especially if you *said* you'd be praying.

Paul described it as being "on the alert." Something we do "at all times." We pray "with all perseverance and petition for all the saints" (Eph. 6:18). Notice how all-encompassing this command and expectation is. The church in Acts 2 experienced life together "day by day." They shared the same purposes, interacting together as if "with one mind."

They were so involved with one another they were constantly going "from house to house" and "taking their meals together," enjoying what the Bible describes as "gladness and sincerity of heart" (v. 46). As a result, despite a rash of persecution and life-threatening challenges in the days that followed, we see God's Spirit working miracles among them. We see bold witnesses for Christ. We see people coming to faith by the dozens—practically every day. We see sin exposed and repented of. We see teamwork. We see abundant generosity and unselfishness. We see regular demonstrations of God's power. We see everything we wish happened in our day, in our churches.

And one of the ways we can contribute most effectively to a revival of church unity today is through the active practice of praying for each other as believers. It heals us. It bonds us. It unites us as one.

Almost all of Paul's letters in the New Testament were written to different churches. But no matter how close his personal relationship with them, he wrote assuring them that he was genuinely, consistently, fervently praying for them.

"[God] is my witness," he said to the Romans, "as to how unceasingly I make mention of you, always in my prayers making request . . . that I may be encouraged together with you while among you, each of us by the other's faith, both yours and mine" (Rom. 1:9–12). He told the Ephesians that he did "not cease giving thanks" for them, "making mention of you in my prayers" (Eph. 1:16). To the Philippians he said, "I thank my God in all my remembrance of you, always offering prayer with joy in my every prayer for you all" (Phil.

1:3–4). "We give thanks to God," he said in writing to the Colossians, "praying always for you, since we heard of your faith in Christ Jesus and the love which you have for all the saints" (Col. 1:3–4).

Our reflex and routine should follow the faithful footprints of this example. Encouraging other believers. Thanking God for them. Exhorting them. Worshiping with them. Bringing their concerns before the Lord, both physical and spiritual. Asking them to do the same for us.

As you think about how to really target this kind of praying, consider a strategy that actually works for all kinds of different settings and different people: using the Lord's Prayer as an outline. Instead of praying it for yourself, pray it for your fellow believers. Something like this:

Father in heaven, I pray for my brother (my sister), praising Your name for them, asking You to fill their heart with worship for You today. May their primary desire always be to advance Your kingdom, wherever they happen to be, whatever they happen to be doing. May they align themselves on the earth with Your will, just as surely as Your will is followed and accomplished in heaven. Provide them, I pray, with their daily bread—with everything You know is required for them to thrive and be cared for. And grant them repentance, forgiving them of their sins—even as You forgive me of mine—while also keeping their relationships free from bitterness and difficulty as they forgive those who've sinned against them. Please, Lord, protect them from temptation, from allowing them to be overloaded with adversity. And deliver them from all evil—from every scheme and attack of the enemy, from every weapon intended to defeat and discourage them. For Yours, Lord, is the kingdom, the power, the glory, forever. You reign and rule and have already given them victory through the finished work of Christ. So I pray for them today, and I pray in His name, amen.

Now that's strategically targeting a prayer. That's biblical praying. That's using the Word—and where appropriate, using your specific knowledge of the person—to aim a prayer in such a way that it covers all aspects of their life and seeks God's will for every bit of it.

Too often, prayer request times between believers become organ recitals. Pray for my aunt's kidney condition. Pray for my cousin's colon cancer. Pray for my brother's big toe. And while we all need and appreciate prayer toward physical health (3 John 2), we must be careful not to prioritize temporary physical needs over eternal spiritual ones. Otherwise, as one man said, we will spend more time praying to keep sick saints out of heaven rather than lost sinners out of hell.

The apostle Paul prayed powerful prayers for believers, almost always aiming at spiritual issues. If you study Ephesians 1 and 3, Philippians 1, and Colossians 1, you will see that he strategically prayed to God the Father, through Jesus Christ, that He through the Holy Spirit would powerfully work deep in the hearts of the saints to reveal the truth of who God is, who they were in Christ, of the great blessings and powerful rewards they already possessed because of their position in Christ. Paul prayed for God to reveal His will and love, to strengthen and equip them toward spiritual fruitfulness and for them to increase in their knowledge of God and faithfulness to God. We can learn so much about how to pray for one another. Many side and secondary issues will get cleaned up and dealt with when the spiritual issues get resolved.

Think of how a commitment to prayer for our fellow believers could energize our relationships and our shared sense of mission. Think of how much more glory God could receive, and how many more answers to prayer we'd see, if He knew the reports would be going out with praise and thanks to all the people who've been praying for us. Think of times when other people's prayers for you—maybe even just *one* person praying for you—picked you up and kept you going. Think of what all we're missing by not taking advantage of this readily available opportunity to bless and be blessed. What a simple investment with such incredible dividends.

Economists, playing off a recent anniversary of the 1980s arcade game Pac-Man, compared the different results a person could have seen, depending on whether they'd placed a quarter into the game slot or into a savings fund. Turns out that when people were investing twenty-five cents into a few minute's entertainment in 1980, the cost wasn't only twenty-five cents. The same monetary value, if placed into a brokerage account on one of the higher stocks in the S&P 500, would currently be worth more than $1,800. If those same people, in pursuit of a high score, had dropped as much as $100 into the machine over the course of the summer, their $100 waste of time could now potentially be worth nearly three-quarters of a million dollars.

How much of our time has been eaten up by little more than our own gripes, our own problems, and our own tirades, when it could've been invested instead in praying for others—with no loss to how God helped us deal with our own life and its issues? What kind of opportunity cost are we actually clamping on to the body of Christ by not giving ourselves more fully—even minimally—to the common cause? "Pray for one another" (James 5:16).

It will pay high, eternal dividends.

Lord, thank You for the church You've given me, and for the friends and families You've enabled me to know through our shared faith in Christ. I pray You would cement our relationships even further by helping us commit to pray for one another. Lord, be pleased by how we love and care for each other. May Your name be glorified as You work in our midst. We will be watching You, and we will be praising You. Bless us, I pray, that the world will see Your power and the difference You make in our lives.

32

PRAYING FOR FAMILY

I have no greater joy than this, to hear of my
children walking in the truth. (3 John 4)

Surely by now, you're way past the kind of praying that's content with only asking God to "bless" and "be with" your spouse, children, extended family, and even yourself. Shouldn't there be more dedicated focus to your praying than that? Shouldn't you know what you're really asking Him for? Specifically? General prayers can get general answers. But we will praise God more and recognize His handiwork when we pray specifically.

So begin assembling a plan from the ingredients you've been gathering along the way—a battle plan for engaging in prayer for the people you love.

For those who are married, this should start with your wife or husband. Marriage is presented in Scripture as more than a romantic attachment that plunges into a life-long commitment. Your marriage is a flesh-and-blood representation of the gospel to your children, your friends, to everyone who knows you. That's why husbands are told to "love your wives, just as Christ also loved the church and gave Himself up for her" (Eph. 5:25). Wives are told to be "subject to your own husbands," not out of any sense of subservience or inferiority, but to support their leadership "as to the Lord" (v. 22), honoring them the way each of us honors our ultimate Head, Jesus Christ.

So you should pray that both of you would maintain a sense of protective passion for this primary function of your marriage. That Christ would be where you run for love, joy, and peace, not your spouse. And then you can bring the love, joy, and peace you gain from Him back to your mate as a gift to your marriage. When disagreements occur, pray that neither of you will allow these differences to dominate, not letting them cause you to lose your first love and focus. Pray that you'll each be committed to listening respectfully, confessing openly, and extending patience and kindness promptly. Hard to offend. Quick to forgive. When outside pressures heat up, threatening your shared commitments to one another, pray that you'll hold firm to your unity at all costs. Pray that God blesses your daily delight in one another and marital intimacy. The example you're setting is too valuable—much more valuable than any perceived benefits that can be gained by letting other people's voices grow more important to you than your spouse's.

On an individual basis—as you pray specifically for your wife or husband—remember from Scripture that our number-one command is to "love the Lord your God with all your heart, and with all your soul, and with all your strength, and with all your mind," followed at a close second by the command to love "your neighbor as yourself" (Luke 10:27). Pray, then, that your spouse would above all be devoted to Christ in loving gratitude, surrendered to following His Word and His lordship. Pray also that each of his or her relationships would be marked by love and unselfishness, especially those that perhaps are the most noticeably strained and contentious right now. Pray for peace. Pray for healing and restoration wherever brokenness exists.

Perhaps next in line, since their discernment of God's will is foundational to living out their purpose, pray that God would keep them vividly aware of His desires, knowing how to handle each day's decisions. Pray that His Spirit would keep you actively and accurately attuned to their needs so that He can employ *you* as a helpful voice of clarity and insight in all their decision-making. Ask Him to give them a fresh delight in seeing the Lord glorified through their lives, so that your prayer for them can echo that of David's: "May He give you what your heart desires and fulfill your whole purpose" (Ps. 20:4).

Already, of course, you can see how these individual prayers extend naturally to your children as well. Praying for God to be first in their allegiance. Praying for their relationships to be strong, supportive, and free of discord. Praying for His Word and His will to be clear to them.

And from there, the Lord will continue to guide you as you grow more specific in your praying. As with your spouse, for example—and with you—Satan is heavily invested in causing your kids confusion, distraction, unnecessary pressure, and doubts about their sense of worth and identity. Your role as a mom or dad is to stand in the gap, attentively listening to them, knowing the true condition of their hearts. Praying *with* them, with your arm around them, as well as when they're not physically present with you. Be diligent in interceding to the Father for their protection, their character, their friendships, their ability to stand up to temptation. They may not yet realize just how seriously the warfare is being waged against them, how many layers of spiritual opposition are working to claim their eye and interest (Eph. 6:12). But *you* know it. *You've* felt it. So don't fail to press into that place where you're defending them in prayer and claiming God's promises of victory in their lives.

If your kids are still young, this means many of those significant decisions and milestones of life are still out there in front of them: educational choices, marriage, job options, as well as significant moments of spiritual decision and commitment. Be praying already for God's Spirit to be going ahead of them, preparing a godly spouse for them, surrounding them with godly influences, planning opportunities in advance where God can utilize their gifts and talents to draw praise to Him as well as drawing other people to Him.

Maybe your kids are grown—with kids now of their own. Pray then, as Scripture so often teaches, that they would remain faithful to God in their generation, enjoying the blessings of "His covenant and His lovingkindness to a thousandth generation" as they and their families continue to "love Him and keep His commands" (Deut. 7:9). And just as you say "Father, I lift up my children," there is nothing holding you back from also adding "and my grandchildren and great-grandchildren" to what you're about to pray. God is not worried or overwhelmed by your prayers reaching out into future generations.

The psalmist was thinking multi-generationally when he said, "That the generation to come might know, even the children yet to be born, that they may arise and tell them to their children, that they should put their confidence in God and not forget the works of God, but keep His commandments" (Ps. 78:6–7).

Again, God's Spirit will steadily unlock the Word so that you can pray for your family and future generations according to His perfect plan for them. You'll never need to worry anymore that you can't think how to pray effectively and specifically for them. This battle plan of prayer for your family is merely awaiting your dedicated intention to be devoted to it. To make a priority of it. To draw them into the bull's-eye of a deliberate prayer target, and to wrap them in ring after ring of focused, personal, Spirit-inspired topics of desire and declaration.

You can (and should) make all kinds of investments in your marriage, your children, and family. Investments of love and time. Physical and emotional support. Carpooling and counseling. Sweat equity and financial generosity. But based on the testimony of Scripture, your investment in prayer on their behalf is the leading, most effective use of your influence. Prayer will help you to better know God while also better knowing each member of your family. They have no better friend or companion in life than a praying husband or wife, parent or grandparent, or whatever wonderful role you've been called to play.

Lord, I bring my family before You today—their needs, their struggles, their goals, their concerns, their present, their future. These loved ones of mine are actually Yours, Lord, and You have graciously shared them with me. Help me best express my gratitude to You by never failing to pray for them, to seek Your will for them, and to ask for Your wisdom as I relate in love and loyalty toward them. Give me discernment as to their physical and spiritual needs in each season, and help me faithfully lift them up to You in faith, love, and in the power of the Holy Spirit. May many generations be blessed because of my prayers. In Jesus' name I pray, amen.

33

PRAYING FOR AUTHORITIES

Remind them to be subject to rulers, to authorities . . .
showing every consideration for all men. (Titus 3:1–2)

ctions and decisions made by people in authority create a significant impact on those within their sphere of influence—both good and bad. Think of a business owner who leads with integrity and excellence, as opposed to one who cuts corners, breaks laws, and routinely passes blame. Think of a father who loves, supports, and wisely trains his children, compared with one who ignores or abuses them. Think of biblical examples like Moses and Aaron, leaders of ancient Israel, whose different ways of responding to God at Mount Sinai resulted in the Ten Commandments on one hand and a golden calf on the other. Our authorities either *help* us in doing the will of God, or they make it *harder* for us to pursue.

Since the influence of people in these positions can cause such a ripple effect, and because their various roles are fraught with hard choices and difficulty, the Bible commands us to pray for all those in leadership over us. "Entreaties and prayers, petitions and thanksgivings . . . for kings and all those who are in authority, so that we may lead a tranquil and quiet life in all godliness and dignity" (1 Tim. 2:1–2). Prayers for their salvation, for their ability to lead or govern, for their commitment to the highest standards and priorities, both personally and professionally.

But while each of us, in one way or another, answers to authorities higher than ourselves—supervisors, parents, officials, law enforcement—most of us also represent some kind of authority over others: children, employees, students, anyone who looks to us for guidance, direction, and instruction. So this biblical command of prayer equally applies to these relationships as well—prayers both for *them* and for *ourselves*, that we who "keep watch over [their] souls" (Heb. 13:17) will take our responsibility seriously and perform it with great care and honor, knowing we will give an account for how we handle the job.

This chapter is intended to help you cover this entire circuit, praying all the way around the whole authority structure, up and down the chain of command. Praying for leaders as well as followers. And all for the glory of God.

We tend to think of authority in terms of organizational charts and the ordinary tasks of each day. But it's more importantly a God-ordained arrangement. "For there is no authority except from God, and those which exist are established by God" (Rom. 13:1). So prayer creates a revolutionary spin on the natural tendency to resist or resent authority. God's call for us is to realize that unless they are asking us to

sin, our obeying of authority (in all other situations) is actually obeying Him. And by praying for those in authority, we
are working in the best interest of everyone.

Authority basically orbits around four centers of activity:
family, church, government, and employment.

In our families, for instance, children should be praying for their parents; parents for their children; wives for
their husbands; husbands for their wives. This is all part
of how God works within a family both to bless its individual members and to make it a force of kingdom influence. Families operate best when following God's design:
"Wives, be subject to your husbands, as is fitting in the
Lord. Husbands, love your wives and do not be embittered
against them. Children, be obedient to your parents in all
things, for this is well-pleasing to the Lord. Fathers, do not
exasperate your children, so that they will not lose heart"
(Col. 3:18–21). The proper ordering of authority within the
home, combined with prayer for one another, strengthens
every ligament of relationship while leading each person to
see themselves as ultimately submitted to the Lord. Caring
and helping one another. Praying for one another. All out of
obedience to Him.

In the church, we're called not only to submit to our pastors and leadership but also to steadily pray for them, praying for their hearts and their submission to Christ so that we
and others can imitate their faith and example (Heb. 13:7).
What a change from the all too typical dislike and disap-
proval of church leaders, whispered and overheard in homes
and back hallways. Our love and support of them is meant

to make their work a joy, which in turn blesses the entire church and its ability to stay focused on its true calling.

But like Jesus did for His disciples and like Paul did for the churches, even so pastors, too, should be praying for their people, feeling a burden of concern for them. They must recognize the gravity of their authoritative role in teaching people faithfully, guarding their hearts, and leading them well under the lordship of Christ, who is the "head of the body"—the One who takes "first place in everything" (Col. 1:18).

In government, as well as in the workplace, the same sort of praying applies. Be faithfully praying for your country's top leaders and elected officials, even those whose views differ from yours, knowing their leadership touches the lives of the many people under their jurisdiction. God still uses imperfect authorities to carry out His perfect purposes (John 19:11; Acts 4:24–28). The Lord, of course, is able to turn the heart of a ruler (Prov. 21:1), and our impassioned prayers and petitions are part of how He does it.

Pray also for your boss and management at work. Like all those in authority, they are charged with these four over-arching responsibilities, among other things: (1) providing direction, instruction, and an example to follow; (2) protecting with boundaries and rules; (3) praising those who do right; and (4) punishing those who do wrong. Let these areas of influence guide your praying. You might even add a fifth—*pointing others to Christ*—because any leader in any job, in dedicating his or her position to God, can be used as a force of spiritual change, both in the lives of individuals as well as the culture at large.

Prayer and authority are a powerful combination. Prayers targeted upward in support of those who lead us, as well as prayers targeted downward for those under our care. "This is good and acceptable in the sight of God our Savior, who desires all men to be saved and to come to the knowledge of the truth" (1 Tim. 2:3–4).

Ultimately, Christ is the reason all things were created, "both in the heavens and on earth, visible and invisible, whether thrones or dominions or rulers or authorities—all things have been created through Him and for Him" (Col. 1:16). So even in praying for people in our offices, schools, and other everyday settings, we are living out a holy calling. It is both highly practical and exceedingly eternal. God is honored by this kind of praying. And because of it, His will is more readily and pervasively done.

Father, I acknowledge that all authority is from You and that all of my authorities only have power because of You. I choose to pray for the biblical, governmental, family, and employment authorities You have placed over my life as a demonstration of my submission to You. Please draw them to salvation and give them a fear of the Lord in all their decisions. Use them to guide, protect, praise, and discipline me in order that I might do Your will, even as I do the same for those under my authority. Use me to be a blessing. Grant me favor so I can daily help people live out their full potential under Your total authority and lordship.

34

Praying for Laborers in the Harvest

*The harvest is plentiful, but the laborers
are few; therefore beseech the Lord of the harvest
to send out laborers into His harvest. (Luke 10:2)*

 Jesus wants us to lift our eyes and see all the people living around us and in the world, and realize they are hurting, empty, wandering, and searching for purpose and meaning, like sheep desperately needing a Shepherd (Matt. 9:36–38). Jesus was moved with deep compassion for them. We should be as well. He commanded us to pray specifically that God, the Lord of the harvest, would send more laborers into His harvest field of souls. Jesus' solution to dealing with overwhelming human needs is prayer—praying for more people to serve in ministry.

This prayer is very strategic and specific. As we pray for God's kingdom to come, we are also praying for more people to seek first and serve His kingdom. Consider this: One man or woman who is completely surrendered to God and filled with His Spirit—who gives his or her life to serve and take

211

the gospel and God's Word to people in need—can radically impact the marriages, families, churches, businesses, and culture in a city. The books of Ezra, Nehemiah, and Esther all show how one person willing to obey God can help shift the direction of an entire nation. Praying that God will raise up more faith-filled kingdom servants is a spiritual bomb-dropping prayer.

Too often we are lost in our obsession with personal needs and entertainment, and we forget the tragedy of spiritual lostness in the world. More people than we can fathom are lost and needing Jesus. Many have heard and received Him. Others have rejected Him. But hundreds of millions still need to hear the greatest news in the world: the gospel. The task is enormous. But nothing is impossible with God. This is His kingdom calling and agenda. That's why it should also be among our highest, most driving priorities and interests in everything we do.

Any follower of Jesus is called to be a laborer in God's "harvest field" (Matt. 13:30; Luke 20:10)—praying, serving, giving, and going. We are joined with an army of others who are already serving here and abroad in their homelands, churches, and adopted countries, each in obedience to this powerful, global mandate. And Jesus calls us to pray specifically for them as well—not just for general blessings, but with strategic passion and focused precision for their most urgent tasks.

Locally, all pastors need an army of prayer warriors in their churches lifting them up. Their work is eternal and vital. Their calling is draining and demanding. The expectations on them are endless. They are commanded by God to be diligent and sacrificial. Devoted and faithful. Passionate and pure. Genuinely seeking to honor the Lord and reach their communities through the serving and equipping of their congregations. Yet the enemy more intensely attacks them. He paints a bright red target on them and their families and tries to wear them down to derail their homes, health, and ministries. Much of their service is visible, but many of their responsibilities are private—laboring in study, providing spiritual counsel, peacemaking a never-ending stream of conflict. They carry a heavy load amid murmuring opposition. So they can grow discouraged and overwhelmed under the weight of a good work. Like Aaron and Hur did for Moses, we should faithfully lift up their arms in prayer, knowing their own strength is not enough (Exod. 17:11–12). They, too, are tempted to sin, quit, or soften their message to appease the opinions of men. That's why they need our prayers. Your prayers. If you want a better pastor, start praying boldly and faithfully for the one you already have. And rally your church to do the same.

Pray using Paul's instruction: "Pray on my behalf, that utterance may be given to me in the opening of my mouth, to make known with boldness the mystery of the gospel . . . that in proclaiming it I may speak boldly, as I ought to speak" (Eph. 6:19–20). Pray for God's protection around your pastor's heart, his marriage, and his home. Pray that he would freely, confidently, unapologetically fulfill his ministry. That he would fear God more than men. That the Spirit would cause many to be drawn to the gospel and grow rapidly into Christlikeness through his efforts.

As you pray for more laborers in God's harvest, go beyond your local church. Pray for other pastors, from other Bible-believing churches, in your community and state. They are also co-laborers with us in this harvest. Pray that the pastors in your city will meet and pray for one another and for the city together—"that the word of the Lord will spread rapidly and be glorified" (2 Thess. 3:1).

Pray for other types of ministries as well—parachurch, campus ministries, family ministries, Christian schools and colleges, humanitarian aid—those doing the work of taking God's Word to all ages, reaching the least, last, and lost around them. Pray that they will be strong in the Lord, "steadfast, immovable, always abounding in the work of the Lord, knowing that [their] toil is not in vain in the Lord" (1 Cor. 15:58).

Then pray for present and future missionaries. Domestic and foreign. Some are starting churches in dangerous situations. Some are introducing new agricultural concepts to under-developed countries. Some are teaching English in foreign schools. Some are introducing orphans to adoptive parents. Some are servicing satellite equipment to spread God's Word. The list is long and wide. But like members of a body, our praying and serving together enables us to magnify Christ in cultures across the globe, as well as here at home, so that His Word and His salvation will be known, embraced, and life-giving. If missionaries could speak as a group, they might appeal, "Devote yourselves to prayer, keeping alert in it with an attitude of thanksgiving; praying at the same time for us as well, that God will open up to us a door for the word, so that we may speak forth the mystery of Christ" (Col. 4:2–3).

Finally, regularly pray for the lost in nations around the world, especially in places where little to no Christian influence is present. By most ways of accounting, the world is comprised of 11,500 different people groups. (*People groups* are those with a common self-identity, based largely on language and ethnicity.) Current data suggests that in more than half of these groups (around 6,800), their populations are less than 2 percent Christian. And half of *those* (roughly 3,200) do not contain any Christians at all and are not being engaged in any way by the gospel. No Bible. No churches. No missionaries. No spiritual light.

We in America, where the message of Christ seems so prevalent, cannot be lulled into forgetting all the nations where His name is unknown. To put it in perspective: the U.S. population is around 320 million. The world population now exceeds 7 billion. America represents less than 5 percent of the globe today. The United States may seem like the center of the universe to many, but heaven will be a vast collection of souls from the world over. "My house," the Lord says, "shall be called a house of prayer for all nations" (Isa. 56:7 NKJV). *God's heart is for the nations.* Our heart should beat along with His heart for the nations as well, "not wishing for any to perish but for all to come to repentance" (2 Pet. 3:9).

So "lift up your eyes and look on the fields, that they are white for harvest," Jesus said (John 4:35), and "pray to the Lord of the harvest to send out workers into His harvest" (Matt. 9:38 HCSB), that "the earth will be filled with the

THE BATTLE PLAN FOR PRAYER

knowledge of the glory of the LORD, as the waters cover the sea" (Hab. 2:14).

Lord, give me Your heart for the nations. A heart of love and compassion for the lost. A renewed love of the gospel and a deep admiration and concern for those who already are giving their lives in service to You. Provide for them, encourage them, prosper their work, and embolden their hearts. Raise up and equip more workers for Your harvest fields. Fill them with Your Spirit, deliver them from the evil one, and empower them to boldly proclaim and represent You and Your Word to the world until You return. Help me be obedient to Your voice and do my part in advancing Your kingdom on earth. In Jesus' name I pray.

35

PRAYING FOR CHURCHES AND REVIVAL

Surely His salvation is near to those who fear Him,
that glory may dwell in our land. (Ps. 85:9)

They started to pray. It resulted in revival. And the praying didn't stop for more than a hundred years.

In May 1727, a tiny band of Christians who'd immigrated to Germany had become known more for their dissension and infighting than their religious zeal. But their leadership began praying for God to move. And five years after establishing their little settlement—revival fell. Bickering believers laid down their gripes and hostilities against each other. People around them were converted by the dozens. Witnesses referred to it as that "golden summer" when God settled down among His people, bringing joy, unity, and the mighty power of the Holy Spirit in His wake.

By August, a young group of men and women, most of them in their twenties or thirties, committed to round-the-clock prayer, each person for a solid hour. Within six months of this nonstop praying, twenty-five people had committed to leave their homes and travel to the New World—the first missionaries of the modern age. The number would eventually grow to hundreds. Along the way, John Wesley would be converted through the influence of this community. He and his brother Charles, along with friend George Whitefield, would be part of massive revival in England. Whitefield would soon make his way to the American colonies, where along with Jonathan Edwards and others, the first Great Awakening would spark to life during the 1730s and 1740s. And the praying in that little German village would continue unabated for more than a century, the fire never going out, as they continued to evangelize the world, changing the shape of whole nations and cultures.

"When God has something very great to accomplish for his church," Edwards said, "it is his will that there should precede it the extraordinary prayers of his people."

Ordinary people praying in extraordinary fashion.

Here at the close of this book, that's our prayer. For you, for us, for the church, for the world. And ultimately for the glory of God. We're here to join with you in fervently asking Him to do momentous, marvelous work in our day. Not just now, not just soon, but for the rest of our lives.

We're tired of caving to the general sense of helplessness about the state of our country and the other nations of the world. The apathy, the fear, the inevitability that no one can really do anything about it. We're tired of disinterested churches making little to no mark for Christ on their communities and neighborhoods, much less their cities and the ends of the earth. We're tired of believers tolerating their own sins, consumed by their own selfish pursuits, content with lifeless religion while millions of people are dying without Jesus.

There's no reason why we can't see God's Spirit poured out in abundance on us, like He's done in days past—reviving families, restoring broken lives. Seeing salvation breaking out en masse, drawing more people to Christ every day. Addictions to alcohol, drugs, abuse, pornography, violence, self-destruction—broken completely away, replaced by a fresh zeal for God and living in spiritual freedom. Racial tensions shattered by the compassionate love and forgiveness of God. Enemies becoming Good Samaritans. Brotherhood among formerly bitter rivals. Prodigals coming home. Crime dropping to historic lows. Churches filled to overflowing by a unified, corporate, acute case of spiritual hunger. The whole cultural landscape transformed.

There's no reason why we can't see all these things—and more. Unless we decide not to pray. Unless we decide not to care. Unless we succumb to the enemy's deceptions instead of believing the proofs and promises of God's Word, calling to us across time, urging us to believe Him again for revival . . . in our time.

Scripture clearly lays out the raw ingredients that have consistently led to revival. "If My people who are called by My name will humble themselves, and pray and seek My face, and turn from their wicked ways, then I will hear from heaven, and will forgive their sin and heal their land" (2 Chron. 7:14 NKJV). "'Even now,' declares the LORD, 'return to Me with all your heart, and with fasting, weeping and mourning; and rend your heart and not your garments'" (Joel 2:12–13). "Let the priests, the Lord's ministers, weep between the porch and the altar, and let them say, 'Spare Your people, O LORD, and do not make Your inheritance a reproach, a byword among the nations. Why should they among the peoples say, "Where is their God?"' Then the LORD will be zealous for His land and will have pity on His people. The LORD will answer and say to His people, 'Behold, I am going to send you grain, new wine and oil, and you will be satisfied in full with them'" (vv. 17–19).

Jesus, in announcing the arrival of His earthly ministry, declared, "The Spirit of the Lord is on Me," with whom He would set the captives free, open the eyes of the blind, and release the oppressed from their bondage (Luke 4:18–19 HCSB). This same Holy Spirit has now been given to believers as well. And He is still able to work mightily in us as God's surrendered people. Jesus said, in fact, we'd be able to do "greater works than these" through His Spirit by choosing to pray and glorify Him with our whole lives (John 14:12).

The secret is united, repentant, humble prayer. Persistent prayer. Extraordinary prayer. Fervent prayer . . . believing that what God wants is always better and more important than what we want.

What God wants are people devoted to Him. People in love with Him. People whose hearts are ready to be used for reaping the harvest. People whose lives are surrendered to His Word. People who are primed to receive the blessings only He can provide.

Evan Roberts, the leading face of the Welsh Revival in the early 1900s, boiled down his message and his heart's desire to a few succinct points: (1) confess all known sin, receiving forgiveness through Christ; (2) remove anything in your life that you are in doubt or feel unsure about; (3) be ready to obey the Holy Spirit instantly; and (4) publicly confess the Lord Jesus Christ. In other words, *pray and obey.* "Bend me" was the frequent prayer that still echoes through the written recollections from those days. And in response to that prayer, God's power came down and set thousands afire with fervent love for Him. "Bend me"—help me to submit, to want Your will first, to follow Your Word without question, to put myself last. To finally die to the vanity of *me.*

So here we stand together at this moment in history. Needing God's Spirit and power to rain down upon us, to work His perfect will through us, to make us ready for everything He desires to do in this generation. Our hope is that every chapter of this book has enriched your relationship with the Lord, equipping you to walk more closely with Him, becoming a more committed and effective prayer warrior.

Let's not just stand here. Let's kneel here. Let's bend here. And let's see what God will do in our midst, in our homes, in our churches, and among the nations. As we press in to prayer. As we unite in prayer. As we fight in prayer.

As we seek Him with all our hearts.

"I will thank you, LORD, among all the people. I will sing your praises among the nations. For your unfailing love is higher than the heavens. Your faithfulness reaches to the clouds. Be exalted, O God, above the highest heavens. May your glory shine over all the earth. Now rescue your beloved people. Answer and save us by your power" (Ps. 108:3–6 NLT).

Lord God our Father in heaven, we need You. We're desperate for You. We pray now in the name and through the blood of Jesus that You would stir up faith and repentance among us like never before. I ask that You would soften our hearts toward You and break our hearts toward sin. Unite Your church in fervency, fasting, and devotion to prayer, desiring nothing more eagerly than we desire You and Your glory to be poured out upon us.

May we humble ourselves, and pray, and turn from our wicked ways, and seek Your face until You heal our land. Have mercy on us, O Lord. Forgive us. Cleanse us. Heal us.

Send revival, O Lord. Bring millions to saving faith in Your Son Jesus. And cause us as Your children to be solely devoted to serving You. Loving You and extending love to others. May the world see Your glory, and may Your name be honored and adored among the nations in our generation. In Jesus' name we pray in faith, amen.

Appendix
Ammunition

RHYTHMS OF PRAYER

The fervent call for revival in the final chapter of this book is not merely wishful thinking. God has poured out His Spirit and moved among cities and nations in times past, stirring up the church and drawing countless thousands to salvation. But He can do it right here as well. In your city. In your country. God usually sends revival on the waves of united, fervent, persistent prayer. The great, known revivals that have left the most indelible marks on past generations grew in the fertile soil of prayer closets and prayer groups and praying churches—often through months and years of cultivation among believers who refused to stop believing that God would hear and respond.

That's why a number of ministries and churches today are championing a united rhythm of prayer, inspired by what was known centuries ago as "concerts of prayer." These involved willing individuals and groups who would commit to regular cycles of prayer, which would then spread to other places where people were following a similar schedule. God responds to the surrendered, repentant, expectant hearts of His people, and He blesses and moves even more when we're working together.

Consider rallying your church to adopt the following rhythm of prayer in the days ahead.

WEEKLY PRAYER—INDIVIDUALLY

At least once a week, whether alone or in a small group, set aside a particular time to pray specifically for revival in your family, in your church, and spiritual awakening in the nation. Pray for the effective preaching and active living of the Word throughout your city during that week.

MONTHLY PRAYER—CHURCHWIDE

Preferably as an entire church body, but at least as a home group, Bible study class, or larger prayer meeting, come together at least once a month in a special meeting for the sole purpose of praying for revival and spiritual awakening.

QUARTERLY PRAYER—COMMUNITY

Consider gathering once a quarter with multiple churches in your area, uniting in prayer for an enormous day, evening, or afternoon of prayer for the spiritual needs of your city. Even if not able to gather together in a central location, simply the understood awareness that churches all over your community are going to be praying together about the same thing, at the same time, would be a powerful experience and effort.

YEARLY PRAYER—NATIONALLY

The National Day of Prayer (the first Thursday of May in the U.S.) offers an annual opportunity for believers across the country to focus as one on revival and repentance, coast to coast. Don't let this day slip up on you or become lost in the day's business. Carve out this time to pray fervently with Christians for revival and awakening in our land.

Appendix 2

Spiritual Temperature Test

Are you hot, cold, or lukewarm? Consider if any of the following statements are true of you. If God reveals sin in your life, then repent and seek His forgiveness and the grace to walk in a renewed, wholehearted relationship with Him in the future.

Indicators of a Cold or Lukewarm Christian

1. When your spiritual life is joyless and apathetic.

2. When you do not love and follow God now as you once did.

3. When you have at least one unconfessed sin that you refuse to repent of.

4. When there is at least one person who has wronged you that you refuse to forgive.

5. When the words of your mouth are displeasing to God and dishonorable to others.

6. When you are not seeing answered prayer or God's power in your life.

7. When you have time for entertainment, but not for Bible study and prayer.

8. When you let pride, worry, or fear stop you from obeying what God has told you to do.

9. When your family sees you behave one way at church and another way at home.

10. When you enjoy viewing things you know are unholy and displeasing to God.

11. When you know people who have things against you, but you make no effort to reconcile with them.

12. When your worship is casual and singing is halfhearted.

13. When your giving is reluctant and calculated, rather than extravagant and sacrificial.

14. When you have to be begged to serve in the church.

15. When you are unresponsive to the neighbors, associates, and friends around you who will likely die without Christ, and you make little effort to share your faith with them.

16. When you are blind to your spiritual condition and don't really think you need to repent or change anything. (Rev. 3:15–19)

Adapted from "When Do We Need Revival? (Fifty Evidences of the Need for a Fresh Visitation of the Spirit in Revival)" by Nancy Leigh DeMoss ©1998 Life Action Ministries. Used with Permission.

THE GOSPEL

God created us to please and honor Him. But because of our pride and selfishness, every one of us has fallen short of our purpose and dishonored God at different times in our lives. We have all sinned against Him, failing to bring Him the honor and glory He deserves from each of us (Rom. 3:23).

So if any of us claims to be a good person, we need to be honest with ourselves: have we ever dishonored God by lying, cheating, lusting, stealing, rebelling against authorities, or hating others? Not only do these sins cause consequences in this life, but they disqualify us from being right before God and living with Him in heaven for eternity.

God is holy, so He must reject all that is sinful (Matt. 13:41–43). And because He is perfect, He cannot allow us to sin against Him and go unpunished, or else He would not be a just judge (Rom. 2:5–8). The Bible says our sins separate us from God and that the "wages of sin is death" (Rom. 6:23). This death is not only physical but also spiritual, resulting in separation from God for eternity.

What most people don't realize is that our occasional good deeds do not take away our sins or somehow cleanse us in God's eyes. If they could, then we could earn our way into heaven and negate the justice of God against sin. This is not only impossible, but it denies God the honor He deserves.

The good news is that God is not only just, but He is also loving and merciful. He has provided a better way for us to have forgiveness and come to know Him.

Out of His love and kindness for us, the Bible says He sent His only Son, Jesus Christ, to die in our place and shed His blood to pay the price for our sins. This provided a pure sacrifice and a just payment to God for our sins and allowed Jesus to receive the judgment we are due. Jesus' death satisfied the justice of God while also providing a perfect demonstration of the mercy and love of God. Three days after Jesus' death, God raised Him to life as our living Redeemer to prove that He is the Son of God (Rom. 1:4).

"God demonstrates His own love toward us, in that while we were yet sinners, Christ died for us (Rom. 5:8). "For God so loved the world, that He gave His only begotten Son, that whoever believes in Him shall not perish, but have eternal life" (John 3:16).

Because of the death and resurrection of Jesus Christ, we have been given the opportunity of being forgiven and then finding peace with God. It may not seem right that salvation is a free gift. But the Scriptures teach that God wanted to reveal the richness of His grace and kindness toward us by offering us salvation for free (Eph. 2:1–7). He is now commanding all people everywhere to repent and turn away from their sinful ways and humbly trust Jesus for their salvation. By surrendering your life to His lordship and control, you can have forgiveness and freely receive everlasting life.

"The wages of sin is death, but the free gift of God is eternal life in Christ Jesus our Lord" (Rom. 6:23).

Millions of people around the world have found peace with God through surrendering their lives to Jesus Christ. But each of us must choose for ourselves.

"If you confess with your mouth Jesus as Lord, and believe in your heart that God raised Him from the dead, you will be saved" (Rom. 10:9).

Is there anything stopping you from surrendering your life to Jesus right now? If you understand your need to be forgiven and are ready to begin a relationship with God, we encourage you to pray now and trust your life to Jesus Christ. Be honest with God about your mistakes and your need for His forgiveness. Resolve to turn away from your sin and to place your trust in Him and in what He did on the cross. Then open your heart and invite Him into your life to fill you, change your heart, and take control. If you are not sure how to communicate this to Him, use this prayer as a guide:

> *Lord Jesus, I know that I have sinned against You and deserve the judgment of God. I believe that You died on the cross to pay for my sins. I choose now to turn away from my sins and ask for Your forgiveness. Jesus, I'm making You the Lord and Boss of my life. Change me and help me now to live the rest of my life for You. Thank You for giving me a home in heaven with You when I die. Amen.*

If you just prayed sincerely and gave your life to Jesus Christ, we congratulate you and encourage you to tell others about your decision. If you really meant it, you need to take some important first steps in your spiritual journey.

First, finding a Bible-teaching church is essential. Tell them you want to obey Christ's command to be baptized. This is a great mile marker that allows you to publicly identify with Jesus, share your faith with others, and launch your new spiritual walk. Plug into your new church and start attending on a regular basis, sharing life with other believers in Jesus Christ. They will encourage you, pray for you, and help you to grow. We all need fellowship and accountability.

Also, find a Bible you can understand and begin to read it for a few minutes every day. Start in the book of John and work your way through the New Testament. As you read, ask God to teach you how to love Him and walk with Him. Begin to talk with God in prayer to thank Him for your new life, confess your sins when you fail, and ask for what you need.

As you walk with the Lord, take advantage of opportunities God gives you to share your faith with others. The Bible says, "Always be ready to give a defense to anyone who asks you for a reason for the hope that is in you" (1 Pet. 3:15 HCSB). There is no greater joy than to know God and make Him known!

God has truly made a way for us to experience assurance and settledness in Him. Of all the things we do not know or cannot predict about life, we can know for certain that He is with us now and that our souls are safe with Him forever.

God bless you as you live out and discover the truth of His promises.

PRAYER STRATEGY VERSES

Prepare to deeply engage in targeted prayer for the important people in your life, using these detailed, biblical plans and prescriptions. Keep them on hand so you can personalize and focus your praying at any moment, enabling you to watch God's answers come to life in response to specific requests. From praying for your family and church leadership, to praying for the lost and the spiritual condition of your city, you'll want to make regular appointments with God in these pages. Not only will you be surrounding your loved ones and others in prayer, but you'll experience Him in amazing new ways.

1. Praying for Your Wife
2. Praying for Your Husband
3. Praying for Your Children
4. Praying for Your Pastor or Minister at Your Church
5. Praying for Governmental Authorities over You
6. Praying for Those Who Don't Know Christ
7. Praying for Other Believers
8. Praying for Laborers in the Harvest
9. Praying for Your City

PRAYING FOR YOUR WIFE (OR YOURSELF)

1. That she would love the Lord with all her heart, mind, soul, and strength. (Matt. 22:36–40)

2. Find her beauty and identity in Christ and reflect His character. (Prov. 31:30; 1 Pet. 3:1–3)

3. Love the Word of God and allow it to bloom her into Christlikeness. (Eph. 5:26)

4. Be gracious, speaking the truth in love and avoiding gossip. (Eph. 4:15, 29; 1 Tim. 3:11)

5. Respect you and submit to your leadership as unto the Lord. (Eph. 5:22–24; 1 Cor. 14:45)

6. Be grateful and find her contentment in Christ, not in circumstances. (Phil. 4:10–13)

7. Be hospitable and diligently serve others with Christlike joy. (Phil. 2:3–4)

8. Bring her family good and not evil all the days of her life. (Prov. 31:12; 1 Cor. 7:34)

9. Invite godly, older women to mentor her and help her grow. (Titus 2:3–4)

10. Not believe lies that would devalue her roles as a wife and mother. (Titus 2:5)

11. Be loving, patient, hard to offend, and quick to forgive. (Eph. 4:32; James 1:19)

12. Have her sexual needs met only by her husband, and to meet his. (1 Cor. 7:1–5)

13. Be devoted to prayer and effectively intercede for others. (Luke 2:37; Col. 4:2)

14. Guide her home and children in a diligent, Christlike way. (Prov. 31:27)

15. Provide no reason for her character to be slandered or to lose confidence. (1 Tim. 5:14)

PRAYING FOR YOUR HUSBAND
(OR YOURSELF)

1. That he would love the Lord with all his heart, mind, soul, and strength. (Matt. 22:36–40)

2. Walk in integrity, keep his promises, and fulfill his commitments. (Pss. 15; 112:1–9)

3. Love you unconditionally and stay faithful to you. (1 Cor. 7:1–5; Eph. 5:25–33)

4. Be patient, kind, hard to offend, and quick to forgive. (Eph. 4:32; James 1:19)

5. Not get distracted or cower into passivity, but embrace responsibility. (Neh. 6:1–14)

6. Become a hard worker who faithfully provides for your family and children. (Prov. 6:6–11; 1 Tim. 5:8)

7. Be surrounded with wise friends and avoid foolish friends. (Prov. 13:20; 1 Cor. 15:33)

8. Use good judgment, pursue justice, love mercy, and walk humbly with God. (Mic. 6:8)

9. Depend upon God's wisdom and strength rather than his own. (Prov. 3:5–6; James 1:5; Phil. 2:13)

10. Make choices based upon the fear of God, not the fear of man. (Ps. 34; Prov. 9:10; 29:25)

11. Become a strong spiritual leader with courage, wisdom, and conviction. (Josh. 1:1–10; 24:15)

12. Break free from any bondage, bad habit, or addiction that is holding him back. (John 8:31, 36; Rom. 6:1–19)

13. Find his identity and satisfaction in God rather than temporary things. (Ps. 37:4; 1 John 2:15–17)

14. Read the Word of God and allow it to guide his decisions. (Ps. 119:105; Matt. 7:24–27)

15. Be found faithful to God and leave a strong legacy for future generations. (John 17:4; 2 Tim. 4:6–8)

PRAYING FOR YOUR CHILDREN

1. That they would love the Lord with all their heart, mind, soul, and strength, and their neighbors as themselves. (Matt. 22:36–40)

2. Come to know Christ as Lord early in life. (2 Tim. 3:15)

3. Develop a hatred for evil, pride, hypocrisy, and sin. (Pss. 97:10; 38:18; Prov. 8:13)

4. Be protected from evil in each area of their lives: spiritually, emotionally, mentally, and physically. (John 10:10; 17:15; Rom. 12:9)

5. Be caught when they are guilty and receive the chastening of the Lord. (Ps. 119:71; Heb. 12:5–6)

6. Receive wisdom, understanding, knowledge, and discretion from the Lord. (Dan. 1:17, 20; Prov. 1:4; James 1:5)

7. Respect and submit to those in authority. (Rom. 13:1; Eph. 6:1–3; Heb. 13:17)

8. Be surrounded by the right kinds of friends and avoid wrong friends. (Prov. 1:10–16; 13:20)

9. Find a godly mate and raise godly children who will live for Christ. (Deut. 6; 2 Cor. 6:14–17)

10. Walk in sexual and moral purity throughout their lives. (1 Cor. 6:18–20)

11. Keep a clear conscience that remains tender before the Lord. (Acts 24:16; 1 Tim. 1:19; 4:1–2; Titus 1:15–16)

12. Not fear any evil but walk in the fear of the Lord. (Deut. 10:12; Ps. 23:4)

13. Be a blessing to your family, the church, and the cause of Christ in the world. (Matt. 28:18–20; Eph. 1:3; 4:29)

14. Be filled with the knowledge of God's will and fruitful in every good work. (Eph. 1:16–19; Phil. 1:11; Col. 1:9)

15. Overflow with love, discern what is best, and be blameless until the day of Christ. (Phil. 1:9–10)

PRAYING FOR YOUR PASTOR OR MINISTER AT YOUR CHURCH

1. That he would love the Lord with all his heart, mind, soul, and strength. (Matt. 22:36–40)

2. Experience the filling and anointing of the Holy Spirit. (John 15:4–10; 1 John 2:20, 27)

3. Honor Christ in his heart, words, and actions. (Ps. 19:14; 1 Cor. 11:1; 1 Tim. 1:17; Heb. 5:4)

4. Be a loving, faithful, Christlike husband to his wife. (Eph. 5:25; Col. 3:19; 1 Pet. 3:7)

5. Lead family and the church with wisdom, courage, and sensitivity that only the Holy Spirit can provide. (Mal. 4:6; Eph. 6:4; Col. 3:21; 1 Tim. 5:8)

6. Abide in Christ and be devoted to prayer, relying on God. (Acts 1:14; Rom. 12:12; Col. 4:2)

7. Rightly divide the Word of truth and communicate the gospel with clarity. (1 Cor. 4:2; Eph. 6:17; 1 Thess. 2:13; 2 Tim. 2:15; 4:2)

8. Have a heart for the lost and be an effective and fruitful soul winner. (Mark 16:15; Luke 10:2; 1 Pet. 3:15)

9. Keep his priorities in line with the will of God. (Prov. 2:5–6; Phil. 2:14–15; Col. 1:10–12)

10. Walk in purity and be protected from the deceptive schemes of Satan. (Eph. 4:27; 2 Thess. 3:3; 1 Tim. 3:7; James 4:7; 1 Pet. 5:8)

11. Create an atmosphere of unity and shared vision for the will of God within your church. (John 17:21; 1 Cor. 1:10; Eph. 4:3)

12. Continue to discover new depths of understanding as a student of the Word. (2 Tim. 2:15)

13. Experience good health, rest, and refreshment from the Lord. (Exod. 33:14; Ps. 116:7; Matt. 11:28; Heb. 4:13a; 3 John 2)

14. Emulate the grace, strength, and compassion of the Good Shepherd toward all those he leads. (Lam. 3:32; Mark 6:34)

15. Exhibit love, comfort, and encouragement as he performs weddings, funerals, and counseling. (2 Cor. 1:3–4; 1 Thess. 5:14)

PRAYING FOR GOVERNMENTAL AUTHORITIES OVER YOU

1. That they would be blessed, protected, and prosperous in their role. (3 John 2)

2. Submit to the authority and ways of God and His Word daily. (1 Pet. 2:13–17)

3. Come to the knowledge of Christ and surrender to His lordship. (1 Tim. 2:4)

4. Lead with honor, respect, wisdom, compassion, and godliness. (1 Tim. 2:2)

5. Use good judgment, pursue justice, love mercy, and walk humbly with God. (Mic. 6:8)

6. Walk in integrity, keep their promises, and fulfill their commitments. (Ps. 15; 112:1–9)

7. Not get distracted or cower into passivity, but embrace responsibility. (Neh. 6:1–14)

8. Watch over, protect, lead, and serve those in their care. (Heb. 13:17)

9. Respect all people without regard to their gender, race, religion, or social status. (1 Pet. 2:17)

10. Hate evil, pride, injustice, and turn away from Satan's lies and schemes. (1 Pet. 5:8)

11. Establish rules and laws that honor God's law and strengthen families and cities. (Deut. 10:13)

12. Reward those who do right and punish those who do wrong. (Rom. 13:1–5; 1 Pet. 2:14)

13. Refuse to take a bribe or allow favoritism in judgment. (Ps. 15)

14. Become hard workers who faithfully fulfill their duties. (Prov. 6:6–11; Luke 12:42–44)

15. Make choices based upon the fear of God, not the fear of man. (Ps. 34; Prov. 9:10; 29:25)

16. Be a godly example in their roles and responsibilities. (Josh. 24:15)

PRAYING FOR THOSE WHO DON'T KNOW CHRIST

1. That God would connect them to genuine believers and the simplicity of the gospel. (Rom. 1:16; 1 Tim. 2:5–6)

2. Disconnect them from influences that are pulling them away from Christ. (John 7:47–52)

3. Expose the lies they've believed that have kept them from Christ. (2 Cor. 4:4)

4. Show mercy, bind Satan, and turn them from darkness to light so they may receive forgiveness of sins. (Luke 19:10; Acts 26:18)

5. Enlighten them to everything God extends toward those who believe. (Eph. 1:17–19)

6. Convict them of sin, God's coming judgment, and their need for a Savior. (John 3:18; 16:8–9; 1 Cor. 1:18; Eph. 2:1)

7. Grant them a repentant heart that turns fully to Christ. (2 Tim. 2:25–26; 2 Pet. 3:9)

8. Save them, change their hearts, and fill them with God's Spirit. (Ezek. 36:26; John 3:16; Eph. 5:18)

9. Help them be baptized and get plugged into a Bible-teaching church. (Matt. 28:18–20)

10. Grant them grace to repent of daily sins and walk in holiness. (2 Cor. 6:17; Eph. 5:15–18)

11. Grow them in Christ by helping them obey the Word of God as a disciple. (John 8:31–32)

12. Help them live with Christ as their hope and true source of peace and happiness. (John 4:10–14)

13. Deliver them from evil, the devil's traps and schemes, and any strongholds. (2 Cor. 10:4–5)

14. Help them abide in Christ and live according to His will. (John 15:1–17)

15. Find them faithful when they stand before God. (Matt. 25:21; 1 Tim. 1:12; 2 Tim. 4:7)

PRAYING FOR OTHER BELIEVERS
(OR YOURSELF)

1. That they would fully surrender their lives to the lordship of Jesus Christ. (Rom. 10:9–10; 12:1–2)

2. Be baptized and stay in fellowship, service, worship, and growth at a Bible-teaching church. (Matt. 22:36–40; 28:18–20; Acts 2:38)

3. Learn to abide in Christ, be filled with His Spirit, and live according to His will. (John 15:1–17)

4. Grow in Christ and obey the Word of God as a disciple. (John 8:31–32)

5. Love the Lord with all their heart, mind, soul, and strength. (Matt. 22:36–40; Luke 6:46–49)

6. Walk in love, kindness, and favor with the lost and believers around them. (Col. 4:5–6)

7. Find their identity and satisfaction in Christ rather than anything else. (Ps. 37:4; Eph. 1:3–14; 1 John 2:15–17)

8. Know the hope, riches, and power of their inheritance in Christ. (Eph. 1:18–19)

9. Be devoted to prayer in secret and corporately in the church. (Matthew 6:6; 18:19–20; Col. 4:3)

10. Repent of daily sins and walk in holiness before God. (2 Cor. 6:17; Eph. 5:15–18)

11. Break free from any bondage, stronghold, or addiction in their lives. (John 8:31, 36; Rom. 6:1–19, 2 Cor. 10:4–5)

12. Walk in integrity, keep their promises, and fulfill their commitments. (Ps. 15; 112:1–9)

13. Live with Christ as their hope and true source of peace and happiness. (John 4:10–14)

14. Share the gospel and faithfully make disciples of others in their lives. (Matt. 28:18–20)

15. Be found faithful when they stand before God. (Matt. 25:21; 1 Tim. 1:12; 2 Tim. 4:7)

PRAYING FOR LABORERS
IN THE HARVEST

1. That God would open the eyes of believers and give them hearts of love and compassion for the lost. (Matt. 9:27–28; John 4:35; Rom. 5:5; 10:1)

2. Call out a new generation into ministry and service of God's kingdom. (Matt. 9:38)

3. Give them faith, courage, and initiative to obey God's call. (Mark 13:10–11)

4. Provide prayer, encouragement, and resources to undergird their work spiritually and financially. (Isa. 56:7; Phil. 4:18–19)

5. Help them serve in the power of God's Spirit and not in the flesh. (John 15:4–10; Gal. 5:16–25; 1 John 2:20, 27)

6. Help them represent Christ well in their words and actions. (Ps. 19:14; 1 Cor. 11:1; 1 Tim. 1:17)

7. Make them diligent, effective, and fruitful laborers. (Prov. 6:6–11; Mark 16:15; 1 Pet. 3:15)

8. Undergird them with the ongoing support and accountability to keep them effective. (2 Cor. 8:1–7; Heb. 3:13)

9. Lead them to abide in Christ and be devoted to prayer, relying on God. (Acts 1:14; Rom. 12:12; Col. 4:2)

10. Grant them good health, rest, and refreshment from the Lord. (Exod. 33:14; Matt. 11:28; 3 John 2)

11. Bless them with strong marriages and families amid the hard work of ministry. (Eph. 5:22–6:4; 1 Tim. 3:4–5)

12. Empower them to effectively evangelize and make disciples of Christ. (Matt. 28:18–20)

13. Help them start churches and establish good leadership in each one. (Titus 1:5)

14. Use them as a catalyst of unity and revival wherever they go and serve. (2 Chron. 7:14; Ps. 133)

15. Help them be found faithful when they stand before God. (Matt. 25:21; 1 Tim. 1:12; 2 Tim. 4:7)

PRAYING FOR YOUR CITY

1. That God would bless your city and make it a safe and prosperous place for families to freely live, grow, worship, and serve Him with their lives. (Psalm 122:6–9, 3 John 2)

2. Raise up strong pastors and healthy churches throughout the city to be a light and a spiritual force for good. (Matt. 5:16; Acts 16:4–5)

3. Open the eyes of believers with hearts of love and compassion for the lost. (Matt. 9:27–28; John 4:35; Rom. 5:5; 10:1)

4. Unite local pastors in prayer for one another and for revival and restoration in their city. (Col. 4:3; 2 Tim. 1:8)

5. Unite churches in prayer, the preaching of the Word, and in serving the needs of their city. (2 Tim. 4:1–3; Titus 3:14)

6. Give our leaders guidance and understanding, and help them fear God rather than man. (Deut. 10:12; James 1:5)

7. Replace poor, corrupt government leaders with strong, godly leaders who will honor God and serve the people wisely, justly, and unselfishly. (Ps. 101:7–8, Micah 6:8)

8. Shut down the corrupt businesses and organizations that are destroying the community with sinful products or practices. (Ps. 55:9–11)

9. Bring in strong, healthy businesses that will benefit families and the city. (Prov. 28:12)

10. Rebuke satanic influences and control over the city, and overcome any strongholds of the enemy with the gospel, prayer, and the blood of Jesus. (Eph. 6:12–20, Rev. 12:11)

11. Replace corrupt laws and standards with just and godly ones. (Deut. 16:19–20)

12. Strengthen the marriages, parenting, and families in the city. (Ps. 112:1–9; 128; Eph. 5:22–6:4)

13. Strengthen the law enforcement to protect the people and eliminate crime. (Rom. 13:1–5)

14. Pour out His Spirit and bring revival to the church and spiritual awakening to the city. (2 Chron. 7:14)

SPIRITUAL AMMO

Verses to use when wrestling with:

Anger
Rom. 12:19–21; 1 Cor. 13:4–5; Eph. 4:26–27; James 1:19–20

Bitterness/Unforgiveness
Matt. 6:14–15; 18:21–22; Mark 11:25; Eph. 4:32; Heb. 12:14–15

Depression
1 Kings 19; Pss. 30:5; 42; 103; 143:7–8; Phil. 4:4–7; 1 Thess. 5:16–18

Doubting Salvation
John 1:12; 3:16; Rom. 10:9–10, 13; Eph. 2:8–9, 1 John 2:20–25; 5:13

Fear
Pss. 23:4; 27:1; 34:4; 91:1–2; Prov. 1:33; 3:21–26; Matt. 10:28; 2 Tim. 1:7

Feeling Unloved
John 3:16; 15:9, 12–13; Rom. 5:8; Eph. 3:17–19; 1 John 3:1; 4:9–11

Greed
Ps. 37:4; Prov. 25:16; 28:22; 1 Tim. 6:6–10

Guilt/Condemnation
Ps. 32; Rom. 8:1–2; 1 John 1:9

Hopelessness
Ps. 31:24; Eccles. 9:4; Matt. 12:21; 1 Cor. 9:10; 13:7, 13; Eph. 1:12, 18; 2:12–13

Lack of Faith
Ps. 34:8; Prov. 3:5–6; Jer. 33:3; Matt. 17:19–20; 19:26, Heb. 11:1, 6; James 5:16

Low Confidence
Deut. 31:6; Josh. 1:9; 1 Chron. 19:13; Ps. 27:1–4, 14; Phil. 4:13

Lust
Job 31:1; Prov. 6:25; Matt. 5:28; Gal. 5:16; Phil. 4:8; 2 Tim. 2:22; James 1:14

Pride
Ps. 10:4; Prov. 6:16–17; 8:13; 16:18; Rom. 12:3; James 4:6–10; 1 John 2:16

Self-Rejection
Gen. 1:26–28; Ps. 139:1–14; Eph. 1:1–6; 1 John 2:20–25; 5:13

Weakness
Psalm 6:2; 79:8; Matt. 8:17; 26:41; Rom. 8:26

Worry
Matt. 6:25–28; Mark 4:19; 13:11; Luke 12:11; Phil. 4:6–7, 13, 19

APPENDIX 6

THE NAMES OF GOD

OLD TESTAMENT HEBREW NAMES FOR GOD

Elohim (the strong Creator God)—Gen. 1:1–2

El Elyon (God most high)—Gen. 14:18; Ps. 78:56; Dan. 3:26

Adonai Jehovah (Lord God)—Deut. 3:24

El Shaddai (God Almighty)—Gen. 17:1; Ezek. 10:5

El Roi (God who sees)—Gen. 16:13

El Bethel (God of the house of God)—Gen. 35:7

El Kanna (jealous God)—Exod. 20:5

Jehovah (the relational God)—Gen. 2:4

Jehovah-Eli (the Lord my God)—Ps. 18:2

Jehovah-Elohim (Lord God)—Gen. 3:9–13, 23

Jehovah-Jireh (the Lord will provide)—Gen. 22:8–14

Jehovah-Nissi (the Lord our banner)—Exod. 17:8–15

Jehovah-M'kaddesh (the Lord our sanctifier)—Exod. 31:13; Lev. 20:7–8; Deut. 14:2

Jehovah-Shalom (the Lord our peace)—Judg. 6:24

Jehovah-Sabaoth (the Lord of hosts)—1 Sam. 1:3, 11

Jehovah-Elyon (the Lord most high)—Ps. 7:17

Jehovah-Raah (the Lord my shepherd)—Ps. 23:1

Jehovah-Rapha (the Lord our healer)—Exod. 15:23–26

Jehovah-Shammah (the Lord is present)—Ezek. 48:35

Jehovah-Tsidkenu (the Lord our righteousness)—Jer. 23:5–6

NAMES FOR JESUS

Almighty—Rev. 1:8

Alpha and Omega—Rev. 1:8; 22:13

Anointed of God—Ps 2:2; Luke 4:18; Acts 10.38

Author and Finisher of our faith—Heb. 12:2

Beloved—Matt. 12:18; Eph. 1:6

Bread of life—John 6:32, 35, 48, 51

Bridegroom—Matt. 9:15; John 3:29; Rev. 21:2

Christ—Luke 9:20

Comforter—John 14:16

Counselor—Isa. 9:6

Creator—Isa. 43:15; John 1:3; Col. 1:16

Deliverer—Rom. 11:26

Emmanuel—Isa. 7:14; Matt. 1:23

Faithful and True—Rev. 19:11

Friend of sinners—Matt. 11:19

God—John 1:1; Rom. 9:5; 1 John 5:20

God of hope—Rom. 15:13

Good Shepherd—John 10:11, 14

Head of the church—Eph. 1:22; 5:23; Col. 1:18

Healer—Matt. 4:23; 8:16–17

High Priest—Heb. 4:14–15; 6:20; 7:26; 8:1

Hope—Acts 28:20; 1 Tim. 1:1

Judge—2 Tim. 4:1, 8; James 5:9

King of kings—1 Tim. 6:15; Rev. 17:14; 19:16

Lamb of God—John 1:29; Isa. 53:7; Rev. 7:9

Light of the world—John 8:12; 9:5

Lord of the harvest—Matt. 9:37–38

Lord of lords—1 Tim. 6:15; Rev. 17:14; 19:16

Lord of peace—2 Thess. 3:16

Master—Luke 5:5; 17:13; Eph. 6:9

Mediator—1 Tim. 2:5; Heb. 8:6; 1 John 2:1

Messiah—John 1:41; 4:25–26

Mighty God—Isa. 9:6

Peace—Eph. 2:14

Prince of Peace—Isa. 9:6

Propitiation for our sins—1 John 2:2; 4:10

Resurrection and Life—John 11:25

Righteousness—Jer. 23:6; 1 Cor. 1:30; Phil. 3:9

Rock—1 Cor. 10:4

Physician—Matt. 9:12

Redeemer—Job 19:25; Ps. 130:8; Isa. 59:20

Salvation—Luke 2:30

Sanctification—1 Cor. 1:30; Heb. 13:12

Savior—Luke 2:11; Phil. 3:20; 2 Tim. 1:10

Savior of the world—John 4:42; 1 John 4:14

Shepherd—Heb. 13:20; 1 Pet. 2:25; 5:4

Son of God—Matt. 14:33; Luke 1:35; John 1:34

Son of Man—Matt. 8:20; Luke 18:8; John 1:51

Teacher—Mark 6:34; Luke 4:15; John 3:2

Truth—John 1:14; 14:6

Victor—John 16:33; Rev. 3:21; 17:14

Wisdom of God—1 Cor. 1:24

Wonderful—Isa. 9:6

Word of God—Rev. 19:13

NAMES FOR THE HOLY SPIRIT

Breath of the Almighty—Job 32:8

Counselor—John 14:16, 26

Spirit of Christ—1 Pet. 1:11

Spirit of counsel and strength—Isa. 11:2

Spirit of faith—2 Cor. 4:13

Spirit of fire—Isa. 4:4

Spirit of glory—1 Pet. 4:14

Spirit of grace and supplication—Zech. 12:10

Spirit of His Son—Gal. 4:6

Spirit of holiness—Rom. 1:4

Spirit of Jesus Christ—Phil. 1:19

Spirit of judgment—Isa. 4:4

Spirit of justice—Isa. 28:6

Spirit of knowledge and fear of the Lord—Isa. 11:2

Spirit of life—Rom. 8:2

Spirit of our God—1 Cor. 6:11

Spirit of sonship (adoption)—Rom. 8:15

Spirit of the living God—2 Cor. 3:3

Spirit of the Lord—Isa. 63:14; Luke 4:18

Spirit of truth—John 14:17; 1 John 4:6

Spirit of wisdom and revelation—Eph. 1:17

Spirit of wisdom and understanding—Isa. 11:2

Voice of the Almighty—Ezek. 1:24

Voice of the Lord—Isa. 30:31; Hag. 1:12

NAMES FOR GOD

Consuming fire—Heb. 12:29

Eternal God—Gen. 21:33; Isa. 40:28

Father—Matt. 5:16; Col. 1:2

God of all comfort—2 Cor. 1:3

God of glory—Ps. 29:3

Holy Father—John 17:11

I Am Who I Am—Exod. 3:14

Judge of all the earth—Gen. 18:25

King of heaven—Dan. 4:37

Lord God Almighty—Rev. 4:8; 16:7; 21:22

Strength of my heart—Ps. 73:26

STARTING A PRAYER MINISTRY

Jesus said in Mark 11:17, "My house shall be called a house of prayer for all the nations." Is this true of your church? Is your local body obeying the call of God's Word to "be devoted to prayer"? Every church should place priority on establishing an active, vibrant prayer ministry that undergirds the whole activity of the church.

If this type of ministry isn't already set up at your church—or isn't thriving—perhaps God is using your time in this book and renewed passion for prayer as an catalyst to help strengthen the prayer efforts of your local body.

The goal of a prayer ministry is not to do all the praying for the church, but to constantly train, equip, enable, and organize members to pray continually and effectively for their members, their cities, and the nations.

A successful prayer ministry requires leadership, a vision, and a team to carry out the work. But every ministry of your church would be blessed if your members became devoted to prayer.

They could establish a dedicated War Room or prayer room where individuals or small groups come to spend scheduled time in prayer. Imagine every small group class having a prayer coordinator and every Sunday morning incorporating more united, focused prayer into the schedule. Imagine small groups meeting for prayer and hosting churchwide days or seasons of fasting and prayer, followed by celebrations of what God has done as you corporately seek Him to take charge of everything concerning your church and to move with power in your midst. Imagine every member becoming a trained and active prayer warrior. Imagine believers coming to church every week with amazing stories of answered prayer in their lives. You can be part of how God begins shaping this reality.

Begin praying about it now and talking about it with others. The Holy Spirit is calling all believers deeper into fellowship with Him. And as much as He wants to help us be praying individuals, He wants our churches to become fervent houses of prayer for all nations.

(For more detailed information, see the *War Room Campaign Kit*, featured in the back of this book.)

DISCUSSION
QUESTIONS

Introduction. Did you grow up in a praying home? Did you ever see any clear evidences of answered prayer in your family growing up? If you made a "Wall of Remembrance" in your home, what specific answers to prayer would you be able to share with others?

Chapter 1. Which persons of prayer from the Bible or Christian history inspired you the most from this chapter on the Legacy of Prayer? Why?

Chapter 2. Have you believed in spiritual warfare in the past? How have you fought battles in the past? Where have you seen prayer work effectively?

Chapter 3. Why do you think churches struggle with prioritizing prayer? What would change at your church if your congregation truly became devoted to prayer?

Chapter 4. What is the glory of God? How have you seen God glorified through answered prayer? What attributes of God has He revealed to you by how He's responded to prayer?

Chapter 5. How have you seen prayer help someone to know, love, and worship God? To better understand and conform to His will and ways? To access and advance His kingdom, power, and glory?

Chapter 6. What is adoration? What is confession? What is thanksgiving? What is supplication? Which type of praying do you tend to do most? Least? How do they work together?

Chapter 7. Describe a time when you saw a prayer answered immediately. How about years later? How does the parenting of children help you in understanding how God answers prayer?

Chapter 8. What is your default prayer time and place? What are the top three things that tend to crowd out your prayer time?

Chapter 9. Which prompt of spontaneous prayer would likely remind you to pray the most in the days ahead? What are some other prompts that were not listed that you have used?

Chapter 10. What postures of prayer have you felt the most comfortable with in the past? Is there a biblical posture or type of praying that you have never really tried? Consider trying it this week.

Chapter 11. Did you identify any locks of prayer in your own life? If so, what steps are you taking to eliminate them from your life?

Chapter 12. Which keys of prayer encourage you the most or help you see what prayer can become in your life? What does it mean to abide in Christ? What are the different aspects of an abiding relationship with Jesus?

Chapter 13. How is Jesus Christ and His death on the cross a key to answered prayer? What did the "Seven Indicators of True Salvation" mean to you (page 87)? How did it affect your thinking about your relationship with God?

Chapter 14. What are some of the biggest problems with pride? What does the Bible say we should do to help us repent of pride?

Chapter 15. How does bitterness hinder our churches and our prayer lives? How is love the "perfect bond of unity" (Col. 3:14)? What does it mean to pray in agreement?

Chapter 16. What does Hebrews 11:6 teach us about faith? What are some of the lies people believe that cause them not to pray in faith? What attributes of God help us to trust Him by faith when we pray?

Chapter 17. When you are praying with others, are you ever tempted to pray in such a way as to impress them? Why or why not? Why can it be hard to pray in secret? What are the benefits to praying in secret?

Chapter 18. How do parents respond differently to the requests of an obedient child versus a rebellious child? How might some use prayer as a cover for disobedience? Share with each other something God has been prompting you to do that you may need some encouragement in doing.

Chapter 19. How do prayers that are not immediately answered actually test and build our faith? Share a story of how God answered prayer after a period of waiting. Why is waiting on the Lord actually healthy for us and honoring of Him?

Chapter 20. What are some Bible verses that are most meaningful to you? How could you use them more effectively in your praying? How would your Bible reading and Bible study be enhanced by allowing God's Word to prompt you into prayer?

Chapter 21. Why do you think God's will has often seemed difficult to discern? What does our struggle to follow His known will for our lives indicate about the condition of our hearts? How have you experienced His peace when seeking His will?

***Chapter* 22.** Discuss the balance between praying sinfully or selfishly and praying freely for good things that your heart desires? Share a story of when God answered a prayer that went beyond a basic need and just demonstrated His loving-kindness?

***Chapter* 23.** Why is God's name very important to Him? What does a name represent? Turn to pages 244–249 and discuss which names mean the most to you personally.

***Chapter* 24.** What is wisdom and how does it help us? Share a time when God clearly gave unexpected wisdom to handle a situation. How often do you pray for wisdom? How might wisdom guide your praying strategically?

***Chapter* 25.** Who does the Holy Spirit dwell within? What does the Holy Spirit do in the lives of believers? How can the Holy Spirit benefit our prayer lives?

***Chapter* 26.** Have you ever had someone overwhelm you by lovingly praying for you? What did they pray? How does praying offensively help us avoid evil in the future? What is your favorite offensive prayer passage shared in this chapter?

***Chapter* 27.** What is preemptive prayer? What are Satan's primary tactics to destroy God's children? What does God's Word say we should do when the enemy attacks? Contrast Peter's lack of preemptive prayer with Nehemiah's faithfulness in it.

***Chapter* 28.** Why is it important to have a ready response plan to the devil's attacks? Can you remember and repeat back the entire R.E.S.P.O.N.D. acronym from memory? Which of the seven parts of the plan meant the most to you and why?

***Chapter* 29.** What are the aspects of extraordinary prayer? Discuss as a group some biblical or personal examples of how united, fervent extraordinary prayer has worked powerfully. How is Nehemiah's prayer an example of extraordinary prayer (pages 185–186).

Chapter 30. Who prayed for you in the past that helped draw you into a relationship with Christ? Is it biblical to pray for lost people? Who's someone you know that needs God, someone you want to start praying for? Close your time together today in prayer for those people.

Chapter 31. Why is it important to pray for other believers? Why do we tend to pray for physical needs over spiritual needs? What are some of the things the apostle Paul prayed for other believers? (See Ephesians 1, Philippians 1, Colossians 1.) Close in prayer for one another.

Chapter 32. Can you share any stories of answered prayer in your family? Who in your family has prayed for you in the past? Who are you praying for now? What are the top three things you would love for God to do in your family right now? Consider praying together for these things.

Chapter 33. Why is it important to pray for our authorities and those under our authority (1 Tim. 2:1–7) How might the world be different if believers over the past thirty years had faithfully prayed for their authorities?

Chapter 34. What ministers have greatly blessed your life in the past? Who did God use to bring you to Christ? How might praying for pastors, ministers, and missionaries affect the church in a positive way? How might it instill in the next generation the importance of serving God in ministry?

Chapter 35. What is revival? What different things have led to revival in the past? What do you think hinders the church from praying more for revival now? Read the "Rhythms of Prayer" guide together on pages 224–225 and discuss ideas that might help lead your group or church to become a people of prayer for all nations. What is God saying to you personally about prayer? What is He leading you to do? What in this study has meant the most to you? Close by praying for revival together, using the written prayer on page 222 as a springboard.

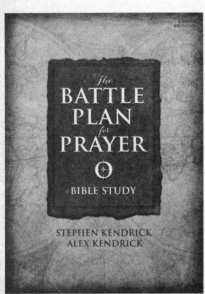

PRAYER IS A POWERFUL WEAPON

Tony and Elizabeth Jordan have it all—great jobs, a beautiful daughter, and their dream house. But appearances can be deceiving. Their world is actually crumbling under the strain of a failing marriage. While Tony basks in his professional success and flirts with temptation, Elizabeth resigns herself to increasing bitterness. But their lives take an unexpected turn when Elizabeth meets her newest client, Miss Clara, an older, wise widow who challenges Elizabeth to start fighting *for* her family instead of against her husband.

BONUS FEATURES

Includes a reading group guide and a color insert with behind-the-scenes movie photos

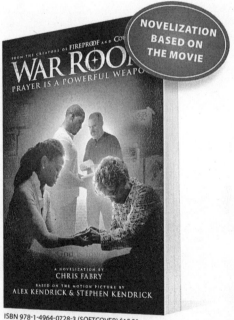

ISBN 978-1-4964-0728-3 (SOFTCOVER) $15.99
ISBN 978-1-4964-0729-0 (HARDCOVER) $22.99

www.WarRoomTheMovie.com

Read the book before you see the movie in theaters August 28, 2015!